A TEMPORARY INCONVENIENCE

AN ORDINARY GUY'S EXTRAORDINARY WALK OF FAITH TO FIGHT CANCER

MARKWIGGINS

innovo
PUBLISHING

Published by Innovo Publishing, LLC
www.innovopublishing.com
1-888-546-2111

Providing Full-Service Publishing Services for Christian Authors, Artists & Ministries:
Books, eBooks, Audiobooks, Music, Film & Courses

A Temporary Inconvenience
An Ordinary Guy's Extraordinary Walk of Faith to Fight Cancer

Library of Congress Control Number: 2018956998
ISBN: 978-1-61314-441-1

Cover Design & Interior Layout: Innovo Publishing, LLC

Printed in the United States of America
U.S. Printing History
First Edition: 2019

DEDICATION

This book is dedicated to Lesa—my caregiver for life!

ACKNOWLEDGMENTS

A special thanks to the folks at CaringBridge for developing and maintaining an excellent communication tool to aid members and their subscribers in staying informed and connected during difficult seasons of their lives.

To over one thousand friends who have followed my journey and have walked alongside us, prayed with and for us—our appreciation knows no bounds.

To those who repeatedly encouraged me to "write a book"— thank you for your gracious prodding. I pray that the seed you watered will end up bearing much fruit.

To founder and CEO of Innovo Publishing, Bart Dahmer, editor and project manager, Rachael Carrington, lead cover designer, Yvonne Parks, and the entire staff of Innovo Publishing LLC for your assistance in making this work become a reality.

CONTENTS

INTRODUCTION 9

WHEN THE BAD NEWS CAME 11

FULL DISCLOSURE 15

WOW . . . I'M NOT ABOUT TO TOUCH THAT 19

MEET NEAL BECKFORD 23

BIOPSY #1 27

SATURDAY MORNING—WHAT ELSE BUT BREAKFAST AT MCDONALD'S? 29

CELEBRATING EASTER 33

THE FIRST DIAGNOSIS 35

ENTER CARINGBRIDGE® 37

    1.   *Care to Go for a Walk?* 41
    2.   *Walk or Workout?* 43
    3.   *Walking with Family* 46
    4.   *Walking with Friends* 49
    5.   *Walking in Faith* 51
    6.   *Walking with Your Mother* 54
    7.   *Walking . . . out of Control* 56
    8.   *Walking in a Marathon* 59
    9.   *Walking in Place* 62
    10. *Walking in the Power of Words* 65
    11. *Walking in a Storm* 67
    12. *Walking in His Faithfulness* 70
    13. *Walking in His Protection* 73
    14. *Walking in the Dark* 75
    15. *Walking with Confidence* 79
    16. *Walking with the Team* 84
    17. *Surgery Day Recap* 88
    18. *Independence Day* 90
    19. *Walking . . . Blessed* 93
    20. *Walking in Praise* 95

21. Walking Again . . . Albeit Slowly 98
22. Walking Again . . . Picking Up the Pace 101
23. Walking into the Unknown 104
24. Walking in Prayer 106
25. Walking in Truth 108
26. Walking with Help 110
27. Walking with Understanding 112
28. Walking in Memphis 114
29. Walking with Christmas Cheer 119
30. Walking and Winning 121
31. Caution . . . CURVE AHEAD 124
32. Walking a Different Path 126
33. Walking Like a Child 128
34. Walking in Day-Tight Compartments 131
35. Walking Blessed, Part II 135
36. Walking with Patience 137
37. Walking with Disappointment 140
38. Walking Directionally Challenged 144
39. Walking on a Balance Beam 147
40. Walking with Memories 150
41. Walking . . . into a Blind Curve 155
42. Walking with a Gamma Knife 159
43. Walking in Thanksgiving 163
44. Walking in Disappointment 165
45. Walking . . . in Search of Miracles 167
46. Walking for a Second 171
47. Walking . . . with Hope! 175
48. Walking . . . and Winning! 178
49. Walking . . . in Need of Water 180
50. Walking . . . to Bethlehem 183
51. Walking (Falling) with Grace 186
52. Walking . . . No, DRIVING! 190
53. Walking . . . to a Place I've Been Before 193
54. Walking in Celebration! 195
55. Walking . . . to My Place in Line 198
56. Walking with a Blood Clot 201
57. Walking and Looking Back 205

THE FINAL CHAPTER 207

INTRODUCTION

I t was the phone call that no daughter should ever have to make to her father. I could hear her on the other end of the phone as she took a deep breath to steady herself for the dreadful message she was about to deliver. She strained for the words, and they quivered as she somehow managed to force them out.

"Daddy . . . the test results show that you have a mass in the parapharyngeal space in your neck and head." It was at that point that the professionalism of the nurse practitioner gave way to the tenderhearted compassion of my baby girl, and the tears she'd managed to temporarily dam up burst forth with uncontained fury. It was not the first time that she'd found herself as the bearer of such news. But this was different—this was her daddy.

I immediately went into "protection mode," trying to console her—albeit from a distance and over a cell phone, which gave very little solace. But the curse of having a medical professional with four degrees in the family leaves you with very few cards to play at a time like this. She understood the gravity of the situation far better than I. Clearly she had researched my case thoroughly, and the news that she was passing on only confirmed what she had suspected for months before.

It was really no surprise to either of us. All of the indicators were there. But now the reality of what we'd feared was upon us. Mass, tumor, growth—all descriptors seemed to be a vain attempt to sugarcoat the situation; but the fact was quickly becoming evident: *I have cancer.*

WHEN THE
BAD NEWS CAME

W ednesday, March 25, 2015, was a beautiful day in Memphis, Tennessee. Spring had made its official arrival the Saturday before, and the weather was already beginning to reflect it in the temperatures. The Memphis Grizzlies were making an extraordinary run for the NBA playoffs, and as season ticket holders, we were finally enjoying the excitement of being in the chase with our lone professional sports team after several, let's say, "mediocre," seasons. Our drive downtown normally takes about thirty-five minutes for a weeknight game. I'd made the trip home from my office downtown, picked up my wife, Lesa, and headed back downtown in hopes of making it in time for the tipoff. That was not looking too promising because I left the office late, and traffic was not cooperating.

Although I abhor texting while driving, I was anxious to hear the diagnostic report from the CT scan I'd had performed the day before. I knew that our nurse practitioner daughter, Whitney, would be combing the electronic records transmissions for the results at the earliest available moment.

While stopped at a traffic light, I grabbed my phone and quickly fired off a text message. Seated in the passenger seat beside me, Lesa just assumed it was a business communication—as it seemed much of my life was either spent with a phone to my head or in front of a computer, and she had graciously grown accustomed to it years ago. When I wasn't talking business, I was thinking business. It was the life of a successful sales executive.

Any word on the CT results? I typed, concealing the phone's screen. No reply. The light changed, and traffic resumed its forward movement.

A few miles later when the phone chimed, prompting an inbound text, I caught the reply out of the corner of my eye.

Yes, was all that it said.

Do we need to talk? I quickly typed back.

I can't.

I could sense the emotion and pain in those simple words. *This is not going to be good*, I thought.

A few more minutes passed—another chime.

I have the girls.

It was making more sense with each text. Not only did she have the results and was reluctant to discuss them, she had her two girls (ages four and two) with her and didn't want them to see and hear her upset.

As we neared downtown, I turned to Lesa and suggested that I drop her at the front door to the FedEx Forum so that she would not miss more of the game while I parked in our office garage. She agreed to my apparent act of chivalry, and soon I was pulling up curbside with the assurance that I would meet her at our seats in only a few minutes. Unknown to her, doing so would allow me the opportunity to talk with Whit in private. I navigated the traffic and in minutes was turning from the alley into our private garage.

The walk from my office to the FedEx Forum in downtown Memphis is only four blocks. I was barely one hundred yards into my trek to the game when the call came. Once she shared the news, the gravity of the situation began to sink in.

I reassured her, "Whitney, it's going to be OK. We're going to beat this!"

"Promise me you will!"

The results also came with a mandate to be in the ear, nose, and throat (ENT) doctor's office on Friday morning to discuss the next steps. I agreed to share the news with Whitney's mother before the night was over (as if you can find an appropriate time for such disclosure; certainly in the midst of an arena full of screaming fans would not be the best choice).

"I promise, baby." And in a moment, the call was concluded.

Although I had continued to walk as we conversed, I now found myself alone on the sidewalk with no one to talk to. Well, not actually. In retrospect it was a rather familiar place—one where I have been before and where, time and time again, regardless the dire nature of the situation, I found solitude in knowing that I was *not* alone. With my head bowed and eyes opened, routinely pondering each impending step on the sidewalk, I resumed my trek as I turned my focus heavenward to pray. Fast-tracking beyond my typical salutations of praise, skipping the lavish words of thanksgiving and adoration, I leapt right into my crisis of the moment! *God, help me to get through this. Whatever the outcome, give us grace to sustain me and my loved ones, and may You be glorified in it . . . whatever path "it" takes us.*

While all of the answers didn't come as to what was in store for the future, I sensed a proven peace that I'd known before and that would mark the beginning of this journey. I took solace knowing that not only was He already aware of my health situation and holding ultimate control over it, He would always be with me as promised in His Word. He was walking with me with each step—not only beside me but out in front of the situation—and also behind me to protect any assaults that I could neither see nor anticipate.

In what seemed like seconds, I was at the doors of the FedEx Forum and was proceeding through security. While to the security personnel, it was apparent to their scanners that I carried no deadly weapons, I laughed to myself as I thought, *If they only knew of the dangerous arsenal that lies beneath the surface of my skin.* The cells in my neck and head were rapidly dividing out of control, and the rental cops were oblivious to my menace onboard.

Making my way to our seats, I was keenly aware that I was about to face my first public test of faith—appearing "normal" to the woman who knows me better than anyone in the world. *It's going to be a long three hours*, I thought.

FULL DISCLOSURE

The Grizzlies ended up being pummeled by the Cleveland Cavaliers. LeBron James put on his usual show, and the twenty-two-point loss for Memphis was admittedly uncharacteristic for this team who had just surpassed a fifty-game win for the season only two nights before. It was the first time ever in the history of the franchise that they'd exceeded fifty wins in the regular season . . . and there were nine games left before the playoffs! It appeared that they were finally becoming contenders. But the loss left us with little to celebrate going home. I was ready to get this over with.

Upon arrival at home, Lesa headed off to get ready for bed. Some time later, I found myself pacing throughout the house, avoiding the ultimate encounter which I knew would mark a key milestone in our future together. You would think after thirty-seven-and-a-half years I would know just the right words to say. But beginning tonight, our roles would change, and our love would be tested as never before.

Finally I mustered up the courage and made my way back to the bedroom. Lesa was already in bed, sitting up with her iPad and no doubt catching up on the latest postmortem report of the Grizzlies' brutal loss. I sat on the bed next to her and, in doing so, immediately gained her attention.

"Lesa, we promised to never keep anything from each other. The test results came back today, and I have a mass in my head and neck." All of the eloquently rehearsed words intended to soften the otherwise brutal news had suddenly vanished. Pausing, I thought to myself, *Is that the best you can do?*

I remember how calm she was—totally uncharacteristic after hearing such a dreaded report and its potentially catastrophic results. *Did she hear what I just said?* I wondered. *Maybe she misunderstood, or maybe I really didn't make myself clear.* After all, many times I have been known to begin a conversation with her after playing out Act 1 in my head without her being privy to said Act or even having been invited to the theater!

Continuing, I shared that even though we knew little at this point, I really sensed God's peace in the midst of this crisis and assured her that "one way or the other," I was going to be OK. Suddenly . . . I had her back.

"I know what that inference means, and you are not going to die . . . do you hear me? That is the last time that you are to say that. You will beat this!"

It was at that moment that the tears began to flow from both of us. We embraced a few moments before voicing prayers and crying out to God for His deliverance. I reassured Lesa that I really did have a peace about the whole ordeal and that I would do everything within my power to win this battle.

Later, as we quietly lay in bed holding each other with only the sound of our mutual breathing, Lesa quietly broke the stillness of the moment. "Mark, I know you are thinking about your mother's cancer, and you can't do that. That was forty years ago, and the improvements in diagnosis and treatment are so advanced when compared with then."

She was right. It was hard not to mentally revisit that place and time. My mother was diagnosed with breast cancer in 1968. As the youngest of three children, I was the only sibling remaining in the household and thirteen years old at the time. Cancer was something that had been totally foreign to me. I'd heard of it, but the only contact I'd had was once seeing a distant uncle proudly show the remaining scars left from his stomach cancer. While I was too young then to understand it or the implications, I distinctly remembered the gross disfiguration of his torso. But I spent my teenage years getting to know cancer up close and personal, and it was very difficult seeing the devastating toll it takes not only on its victim but the reverberating impact that it has on family, friends, coworkers, and others you hold dear.

My mother would live five torturous years fighting breast cancer. Lesa was accurate in her comforting words to me. There have been incredible accomplishments in diagnosis and treatment in the last four decades. My mind reflected on how life could have been different if those advancements had been available then. My mother would have experienced getting to know the woman lying beside me as God's answer to her prayers for her youngest child. She would have held two beautiful girls, and, nurturing them the way she did me and my sister and brother, she would have taken great pride in the wonderful ladies that they have become. The same holds true for my siblings and their children. Cancer robbed my mother of countless memories, and I wasn't going to let it rob me without putting up a fight.

But one thing that *was* available back then had not changed. The faith in God that she'd demonstrated to me over forty years ago was still as fresh (though aged), new and vibrant (though ancient), and current (yet timeless).

I texted Whitney that the news had been delivered and that Mom had handled it better than expected. Perhaps it was still too fresh for any of us to fathom what lie ahead. I told her that I would call her sister, Lindsay, in the morning to tell her the latest because it was so late, but she replied that she had already done so. Figures . . . those two are so close that Lindsay may have heard from Whitney concerning the results before I did. But I wouldn't have it any other way!

WOW . . . I'M NOT ABOUT TO TOUCH THAT

L esa, Whitney, and I arrived at the ear, nose, and throat clinic for our Friday appointment. Lindsay (in Dallas) was impatiently waiting for a phone call once we all learned what the next steps were to be. As Whitney was copied along with the attending physician on the CT scan results, they were aware that we knew the mass was there, which made the appointment a little less ominous. Yes, slightly less ominous . . . but not like going to get your teeth cleaned. Still, a somber mood prevailed with the lead physician and his assistant.

"Mr. Wiggins, the results of your CT scan show a mass in the parapharyngeal and masticator spaces. And based on its size and location, it probably explains both the hearing problems in your left ear that we have been trying to resolve as well as the headaches you have been experiencing."

"OK, where exactly is that?" I retorted.

"Up under here," he said, placing his finger underneath the ridge of my left jaw, "from about midpoint of your chin to the base of your cranium."

"And, next steps?"

"Well, we will need to schedule a biopsy as soon as possible to determine exactly what we are dealing with. But regardless, due to the size and location, it's going to have to come out."

"And you'd perform the surgery?" I asked.

Looking back at the film, he slowly shook his head. "Mr. Wiggins," he said, "I do surgeries of the ear, nose, and throat all the time . . . but *wow*." Looking again at the film, he continued. "I am not about to touch that. There are so many critical nerves, vessels, and structures . . ."

I could tell he wanted to say more but didn't.

"So . . . I will do some additional research regarding surgeons specializing in this type of procedure and will get back to you. In the meantime, let's get a biopsy scheduled. Again, due to where the mass is located, it will be a very delicate procedure, and we'll need to do a guided needle biopsy through your cheek as opposed to simply going in through your mouth. I'll have my nurse arrange the procedure for early next week."

Rather than head back downtown to the office, I headed home to try and get my arms around the situation. It was March 27—my brother, Steve's, sixty-fifth birthday. As much as I felt the need and desire to share my news with family, I just could not ruin his big day with such depressing news. *It can wait a day or two,* I thought, giving myself time to both process this uncharted turn of events and to emotionally prepare for the additional caring questions that would come from loved ones. The weekend ahead would prove to be one filled with a barrage of such questions—who to tell, when to tell, what to tell. At this time, there wasn't a lot that we could tell anyone. I've always been one to deal in facts, and at that moment, there were few facts that we could share.

Because it was midafternoon on Friday when we concluded the appointment, I was not surprised that the call didn't come until the following Monday.

"OK, you are scheduled for 2:00 tomorrow afternoon for your procedure," the nurse stated. "I'm sorry that we're just getting this to you now, but I'd left on Friday before your appointment was over and didn't get the order until this morning."

She gave me the clinic's address where the biopsy was to be performed and wished me well. For her, it almost sounded too routine, and perhaps to her it had become that. But we were about to discover that those instructions would result in a whirlwind of activity, sending us down a different path—one that would show God's hand intricately involved and leading from the start.

Later in the afternoon, Whitney texted from work: *Did you hear back on the biopsy appointment?*

Yes, I replied, sharing with her the name of the practice and the specifics for the next day.

OK, good. We can talk about it more over dinner.

Knowing that this was not a simple procedure, I'd called the interventional radiologist's office to confirm with them the time and their location, and then I asked them if there were any special instructions or preparations needed before the procedure.

"No, just be here a few minutes before 2:00 so we can get your paperwork completed and insurance information."

I found that odd, considering there may be sedation involved. It would mean NPO (nothing to eat or drink for hours before). It could mean that I would need someone to come with me to drive me home after the procedure. *Seems strange*, I thought.

We were barely into dinner when nurse Whitney began with the questions.

"So what instructions did they give for you before you arrive tomorrow?"

"Nothing . . . just show up a few minutes early with my insurance card."

"That doesn't sound right." I could see the wheels turning in her head. "I'm calling them first thing in the morning," she said.

And she did . . .

MEET NEAL BECKFORD

Tuesday morning was going to be an incredibly busy day. I'd arrived at the office early for a major product line review presentation, and my vendors were scheduled to arrive for the meeting later in the morning.

By 8:30 a.m., my phone was ringing. On the other end of the call was a very livid Whitney.

"Dad, not only have they scheduled you for the wrong procedure, they have it with the wrong specialist! I called them this morning, and they told me that instead of a guided needle biopsy, they have you down for a routine ultrasound. They don't even do the biopsies there!"

Now you have to understand a couple of things about Whitney. First, she takes health care and her profession very seriously. It took years of seemingly endless study and training to achieve her level of competency. Besides, we are talking about life and death considerations and the wellness she hopes to see resulting in all of her patients. Second, she will tell you that while no one in healthcare is perfect, you don't go jacking around with her daddy's health plan when there is a monster growing in his head. Do-overs are not an option. Doctor #1, you've just been fired.

"But here's what we are going to do," she continued. "I've got mama going over to pick up your CT scan films from the diagnostics center and taking them to another interventional radiologist who has agreed to read them to render a second opinion. She's en route to get those now. I've already spoken with his nurse practitioner who is a personal friend, and she's going to fast track this with him as soon as they arrive. I'll call you back with what he says when he has reviewed them. Dad, I am furious!"

Ending the call, I got back to work. So much to be done. Besides, I've got to get my mind off of this.

Barely an hour had passed. Lesa called to tell me that she'd accomplished her assignment, and the films were in the necessary hands. As promised and within minutes, a second call from Whitney came.

"While the interventional radiologist's interpretation agrees with the original reading as far as the mass, he disagrees that a guided needle biopsy should be performed because it is far more risky and causes concern for irreparable damage to key nerves and vessels. He recommends instead to do a traditional tissue sample biopsy through your mouth, considering the mass is readily accessible in the recesses of your left jaw. So, learning that, I've also contacted Dr. Neal Beckford's office and explained your case, the urgency, as well as the experience we've just encountered. He can see you in forty-five minutes. Can you be here? Their offices are literally across the parking lot from ours [Whitney's workplace]."

That's thirty minutes of drive time, I thought. "OK, I am on my way."

Rallying the troops in the office, I hurriedly explained that I had to go to an unexpected doctor's appointment, which would most likely mean that I would not be available for the rest of the day—including the crucial meeting that was now only three hours away. They agreed to cover for me and to explain the reason for my unexpected absence to our vendors and the customer. All that anyone could say was that I had to make a necessary appointment with the doctor. After all, at this point, that's all they knew.

It was agreed that Lesa and I would meet at Whitney's office, and the three of us would make the short trek to the ENT group together. Lesa and Whitney were waiting there for me when I drove up just minutes prior to the scheduled time. Whitney had cleared her appointments in order to join us.

She'd referred several patients to Dr. Beckford but had never met him personally. We all expressed our appreciation for him working us into his day with such priority. It didn't take long for us to gain an incredible appreciation for this gifted physician who immediately puts you at ease and instills a sense of confidence in very short fashion.

After a very thorough exam and reviewing the CT films, he quietly and calmly rendered his opinion.

"Well, it appears that you definitely have a tumor as the CT has indicated; however, if I had to make a wager—which I don't do—I'd say it is a schwannoma, which is a benign form that is characterized by a firm, encapsulated mass that is easily removed surgically. We'd just go in and scoop it out, and you'd be good as new. But we won't know that for sure until we have a biopsy to confirm that. And I believe the best and easiest way to do that is to go through your mouth. It is accessible, and doing it this way won't risk traumatizing other surrounding vessels or nerves."

"Would you be the one to do that?" I asked.

"Sure, right here in the office. Let's get with someone to schedule it as soon as we can." He led us to a young lady responsible for appointments. We again thanked him for making my case such a priority, and he was off to his next patient.

She spent a minute perusing the options in her scheduling software. "Looks like the fourteenth of April is our first available appointment," she said.

"That's two weeks away, and Dr. Beckford indicated that this needed to be done as soon as possible."

"That is our first opening," she emphatically replied.

"I'll take it." *Another two weeks before we can do this?* I thought, feeling the anxiety of becoming another healthcare casualty statistic due to the endless waiting. As I stood at her desk and reluctantly began entering the information into my phone's calendar, Dr. Beckford appeared again from seemingly nowhere.

"What about tomorrow morning at 11:00? I have a surgery in the morning that shouldn't last that long, so we can do it then," he offered.

"Great . . . thank you so much," I blabbered—torn between joy and relief.

Walking out of the office, Lesa, Whitney, and I unanimously echoed a feeling of confidence in this turn of events that led us to both Dr. Beckford and the decision to proceed with the traditional biopsy—*and* it being addressed so timely. Lesa and I thanked Whitney for her managing the ugly situation and acknowledged God at work in the events as they had unfolded. We called Lindsay to give her an update and to share in our new sense of optimism.

I looked back down at my phone and resumed entering the information for the appointment into my calendar, careful to include the reminder prompts even though it was now less than twenty-four hours away. Date now changed to April 1 . . .

Wait, a biopsy on April Fools' Day? You've got to be kidding!

BIOPSY #1

We arrived at Dr. Beckford's office the next day, eager to get the tissue samples extracted and his preliminary prognosis confirmed. As promised, I would be his next appointment provided the morning surgery went as expected, and it did. So I was ushered right in and prepped for the procedure, which was simply administration of a local anesthetic to the site where he would be taking the sample.

"This will be easy," he said as he began numbing me up. A couple of injections later and I was beginning to feel no pain. "Let's give it about ten minutes to get the full effect," he commented as he stepped out of the room to gather some more instruments.

The tumor was indeed very accessible. From the time I had first noticed the swelling three months earlier until now, it had continued to push forth into my mouth from the recesses of my left jaw. Chewing had become very difficult, and opening my mouth to any great extent was becoming restricted. On the outside of my head and neck you could not tell there was anything going on. But under the surface, it was a different story.

Now back at my side, Dr. Beckford began taking the samples with the aspirating core tool, a device similar to a large bore shot needle with a trigger that is designed to puncture the tumor then aspirate (suck up) a core sample for pathological examination. I heard the first sample being "spat" into the petri dish from the instrument, then the second—now another.

"Huh . . . I'm not real happy with the viability of these samples, so I'm going to go ahead and cut actual tissue samples as well."

I signaled my approval as best I could, considering my mouth was full of equipment and his hands. I was still all numbed up, so, at the moment, he could take whatever he needed to get the good results we were hoping for.

Cutting into the tumor, I could feel him rip off a piece.

"That should do it," he said, and we were done.

Dr. Beckford explained that it typically took a couple of days to get the pathology results, but due to the second day falling on Good Friday, he said to expect it to be Monday before I heard back from him.

Oh yeah, how could I forget? It was *the week of Easter.* But the events of the last few days had so rattled my brain that everything else had just become an "Oh yeah, we have that going on too."

"Hey, Doc . . . we have our Easter choral presentation at church this weekend. Am I still OK to sing with my mouth in this condition?" I inquired in my best numbed slur.

"When is it?" he replied.

"Well, there's our last practice tonight—just over six hours from now—then performance at the Good Friday service on Friday night—forty-eight hours away—and again on Easter morning."

"I'll leave that up to you . . . just don't overdo it. Whatever you can manage. The sedation will wear off in a couple of hours, and I will send you home with something for pain. Any bleeding should be stopped by tonight's rehearsal."

And it did, and I took it easy for the last rehearsal, looking forward to the Good Friday observance to come two days later.

On Friday morning the original ENT doctor's nurse called, apologizing for the mix-up. "We are trying to reschedule now with the hospital that recognizes your insurance, but they are telling us that because the guided needle biopsy is a surgical procedure, it will probably be another two weeks before they can even tell us an available date to have it done," she said.

I explained to her that we'd chosen a different path and that the biopsy had been performed and we were awaiting the results.

Thank you, God, for leading me to the express lane!

SATURDAY MORNING— WHAT ELSE BUT BREAKFAST AT MCDONALD'S?

As for many families, breakfast at McDonald's on Saturday mornings has become somewhat of a self-proclaimed family tradition. Years after the advertising slogans of my time have collected dust in the marketing department's archives, their impact has lived on with my generation and those to follow. Yes, *You deserve a break today*; *Get down with something good*; *Two all-beef patties, special sauce, lettuce, cheese, pickles, onions, on a sesame seed bun*; *Mac tonight*; *Did somebody say McDonald's?*; *We love to see you smile*; and *I'm lovin' it* have each brought you back time and ceaseless time again.

The small, rural, South Alabama town that was my home débuted the golden arches in the years immediately after the birth of our first child, so as soon as she and (later) her younger sister could eat solid food, we began making our weekly Saturday morning trek on foot (yes, it was only four blocks away door to door). Some of my fondest memories are of the four of us walking together as a family, with the kids alternating turns on my shoulders.

Consistency was something McDonald's had mastered, and they were the model of perfection for food franchising. But while the food was always as advertised, it was their sheer ability to capture and hook the pallet of toddlers and youngsters that was undeniably the key to their success. And it was not with a special sandwich or even the development of the revolutionary Chicken McNugget that was the driver but rather a few pennies spent on a plastic toy from China (which may or may not work) that mesmerized the kids and that sent them salivating for the latest "must have" toy that was being promoted along with the Happy Meal. I can't begin to innumerate the times that I have witnessed untouched food from a Happy Meal as kids mindlessly play with extruded plastic in total oblivion to why they are sitting at the table.

Oh, and if that isn't enough, if you are really lucky, you've landed on one of the locations that has the second pièce de résistance—an indoor entertainment complex and obstacle course that, for a three-year-old, rivals some theme parks. McDonald's learned early on to attract the child and the adult, and their dollars would follow. Even our hometown location had a three-seat merry-go-round that ran for free with the simple push of a button—and that was thirty years ago! So, again, place your order for the Happy Meal (with gender appropriate toy) and head to the play area while the grinning store manager does his happy dance—cha-ching! But if time constraints prevent the full menu of satisfaction for your little one, there is always the drive-through . . . as long as the meal comes with *the toy*.

But the convenience of a drive-through cannot compare with the experience of Saturday morning in the dining room. So it was not unusual that Lesa, I, and Mary Collins (granddaughter number one and daughter of Whitney and Ben) found ourselves there the next morning following the Good Friday service. The tradition is now being experienced by the next generation, and our oldest granddaughter (age four) had grown quite fond of this time alone with her Mia (Lesa) and Pa (me). She'd spent Friday night at our house, and I'd craftily chosen a McDonald's location near to us—but with no noisy playground area—and we were enjoying our feast of pancakes. My cell phone rang, and the screen displayed a local number that was not familiar. I hesitated answering, thinking that it was probably one of those nuisance solicitations that I deplore. I don't know what prompted me to answer, but I did.

"Hello?"

"John Wiggins, please," the rich bass voice resonated. I immediately recognized it.

"This is John [my first name, as in John Mark] . . ."

"John, it's Doctor Neal Beckford. I've received your pathology report, and it's malignant. I'm sorry to have to share that news, but I knew that you'd want to know at the earliest time."

"I see . . . and, next steps?"

"I would like to refer you to a colleague at MD Anderson in Houston. He's a gifted surgeon and, quite honestly, the only one that I would recommend to deal with a case as involved as yours. We can talk about it further in my office on Monday at 4:30 p.m. It's my last appointment time for the day, and we can take time to answer any questions you may have."

I thanked him for reaching out to me and pressed the *End* button on my phone. *Oh, I hope that's not a sign*, I thought.

I looked at Lesa, who'd been trying to act occupied with Mary Collins. She knew by the conversation on my end that something was up, not to mention that my body language was clearly trying to cover something up in front of the grandchild. We made eye contact.

"We need to go . . . ," was all I said.

We hurriedly cleaned the remains of our breakfast and piled in the car. As I drove toward Whitney and Ben's house, the questions continued to roll in my mind like the ominous clouds of a deadly thunderstorm. I was totally numb!

Wait, slow down . . . this is all happening too fast, I thought. *What happened to the benign schwannoma that would be easy to remove? It is a Saturday morning. It is Easter weekend. We were told not to expect results until Monday. What kind of doctor is at his office on a Saturday . . . or a holiday weekend (a good one)? How much more good news can one week bring? MD Anderson (MDA) . . . I've heard of them; they are really good at treating people who are really sick.*

Arriving at Whitney's house, Mary Collins was shuffled out of the car, and Whitney took her place so that she could accompany Lesa and me home and talk more openly. As we drove away, I recounted the conversation with Dr. Beckford as best I could for both her and Lesa, struggling to make sure that I had not forgotten a detail of importance. A much-dreaded call to update Lindsay followed. It would be a long forty-eight hours as we experienced another episode of waiting until we could somehow get more answers. Then the path suddenly turned in a direction we were not anticipating—with something that we would have to begin to cope with as reality began to soak in.

CELEBRATING EASTER

We all began dealing with the news in our own respective ways. One of the things that I attempted to make clear from the start was that life was to go on as "normal" as possible. Yeah, well . . . in theory that was my desire, but I really was not aware of how the coming days would play out, particularly in light of this latest twist.

The next day was Easter. Lesa and I had shared my situation as a prayer request with our Bible study group the previous Sunday, and as strong as her faith was, she said that she was not emotionally prepared to deal with the questions and concern that would no doubt be lovingly poured out on her as the news began to spread among our church family. It would be the first time in sixty years of life that she was not in church on Easter morning, but I told her that I understood and respected her feelings. Besides, on top of everything else, the Memphis family would be showing up for Easter dinner later in the day, and she'd not missed anything in preparation for that. She is a master hostess, and every holiday with her is special.

But as much as I desired to be with her, I felt compelled to go and complete my commitment to the choir. I'd sung in our Good Friday service and honestly felt that I may have blown out my pipes. We'd done a run through of all of the songs once before, and then again for the actual presentation, and my voice was spent. Still, that was Friday night, and I would have had a day of rest in between then and our singing again on Sunday morning.

We debated whether I should push myself and what possible repercussions it could have on the tumor and surrounding areas as it was becoming increasingly difficult to open my mouth wide, to eat, and at times to talk. Finally, with a trembling voice, I told Lesa, "If there has ever been a time for me to sing of the hope that we have in the resurrection, now is it. I have to do it."

What I didn't say was this may be my last chance to sing and participate in a performance of Easter music with our choir . . .

What I didn't say was that the days ahead may be the end to my singing . . . period.

Singing, speaking, hearing—they were all at risk. All I knew was if loss of any of those were to be the case, then I was prepared to leave it all that morning at the empty tomb of our risen Savior in celebration of what He's done for us.

It was a great service and especially meaningful choir presentation for me. I'd made it through, though pausing at times to fight the tears that welled in my eyes.

We returned home for a wonderful meal that Lesa had waiting for us. For the rest of the day, celebration of Easter was far from usual at our house. As happy as we wanted to be, Saturday's news had left us emotionally drained, and a somber mood prevailed as we anxiously awaited in anticipation of more news from Dr. Beckford on Monday afternoon.

THE FIRST DIAGNOSIS

It's a special gift when a doctor cares about the emotions and concerns of spouses and family members equally as much as the patient he is treating. That is certainly the case with Dr. Neal Beckford. We quickly became accustomed to the warm and compassionate interest he took in both wife and daughter each time he entered the examination room. He'd always address them first, spending as much time as needed to reassure them before turning his attention to me. Today would certainly be no exception as he would share with us all in more detail what he'd briefly confirmed in our conversation on Saturday.

"I'm truly sorry . . . it's not what any of us were suspecting, but the pathology report says you have squamous cell carcinoma, and it is stage four as it appears to have spread to the lymph nodes in your neck."

"And you recommend someone at MDA?" I replied.

"Yes. Dr. Jeffrey Myers is a colleague of mine that I believe to be the best choice for you to both perform the surgery that will have to take place and to administer the proper treatment plan. I don't know of anyone in Memphis or even Nashville who can begin to address this better than he."

"Anywhere else you would suggest?"

"Well, there is Sloan Kettering in New York, or the Mayo Clinic, or City of Hope in California, but MDA has everything they all have to offer, and I believe more. If my mother had what you have, I would tell her to see Dr. Myers at MDA. I've already made a call to his office on your behalf."

"OK, let's do this."

"I will let you know as soon as I hear back from Dr. Myers. Meanwhile, if you have any more questions, here is my cell phone number. Godspeed and God bless you, my friend!"

A couple of days later, he did call back with the good news that Dr. Myers had agreed to take my case, and I should report to Houston on April 29 for evaluation.

Great . . . another three weeks of waiting, I thought.

If I only knew . . .

ENTER CARINGBRIDGE®

The Grizzlies seemed to share my depression—going on to lose three in a row before resurrecting from their funk. They went on to have a franchise record year, finishing the regular season at 55-27, defeating the Portland Trail Blazers in the Western Conference First Round before losing the Western Conference Semifinals to the Golden State Warriors, who ultimately became NBA Champs. We made some of the games down the stretch and followed others on TV once arriving in Houston, but suddenly basketball had lost its luster. There was a much bigger game at stake—the game of life.

Back at the office, the team and I formulated a plan for just how and when we would announce the news to our customers and vendors. We divided up my responsibilities and who would contact whom. After all, my plan was to take a ninety-day medical leave of absence, get this fixed, and get back to work. It was to be a temporary inconvenience, nothing more. That was my expectation. That was my plan. The team backed me 110 percent. I stopped once again, as I have many times over the last eighteen years, to thank God for leading me to this position just when I needed it most. While I attempted to immerse myself in my job for those next three weeks, I longed to get to Houston and have this issue addressed.

Once my family got over the shock of my being diagnosed with cancer, one of the biggest additional challenges we faced was how best to communicate with the rest of the family, friends, work associates, and other loved ones in an accurate and timely fashion. So many expressions of love and concern had already been shown that we were absolutely dumbfounded and were feeling a deep sense of gratitude, which permeated our lives from the earliest days of this journey. Scores of people were already praying fervently for our situation, and we believed it our responsibility to keep them informed so they would know how to pray specifically for the needs we experienced at the time. Also, as well intentioned as people are, second, third, and fourth generations of a report can tend to get distorted, misrepresented, confused, etc., so that it somehow reels out of control. I wanted to be able to reach out and honestly share the facts (good or bad) with those who cared and to provide a ready depiction of those facts from the source (me). But I also knew that there was no way I would be able to continue to respond to every text, email, voicemail, letter, card, Facebook post, etc. that was beginning to flood in.

That's where CaringBridge® came in. The only experience that I previously had with the site was during the last days of a dear cousin's husband. It provided me with not only an answer to the above challenges, but it also provided me with a personal firewall that insulated me from the compelling desire to fire off a reply to all of the many acts of kindness that were coming my way and to my family. CaringBridge® became my conduit to what would become a vast following. We communicated the site information to biological family, church family, business associates, and friends, and asked them to forward to others who may not have heard how to connect with us. We even posted the information on Facebook, which, well, like it or not, opened it up to the world of anyone who may be remotely interested.

Lindsay, our tech savvy graphic designer and daughter, set up the site and instructed her dad on how simple it was to log on and make a journal entry. Then, anyone who cared to could read my latest communication and make a comment or offer words of encouragement in reply to my entry—either then or at any time on their own. They could even set their CaringBridge® account so that it would automatically prompt them whenever I would add a journal update so that they would have the latest information.

The responses were amazing and so uplifting. After the first couple of posts, I was so encouraged that I became burdened to have an update ready as often as I could. It actually became a therapeutic outlet for me to write, and the responses were a constant reminder that *no one fights alone*.

I've asked from the start that this journey and its many paths be used for God's glory—that the words that I write be His words, and that those who read them will be forever changed. Those words (His, not mine) have the power to heal not only cancer but more importantly, heal a longing, hurting, Christ-less soul.

So join us now as we walk together . . .

CARINGBRIDGE® JOURNAL ENTRY #1
APRIL 29, 2015

CARE TO GO FOR A WALK?

W ell, fancy meeting you here. I'll have to admit this is the last place that I thought I would be writing you from, but just the fact that you have logged on is evidence of your interest in my journey. So let me begin by thanking you.

We have been truly humbled by the outpouring of love and support since learning of my diagnosis a few weeks back. That support has shown itself in so many ways—from personal encounters, to thousands of prayers offered both on my behalf and for my family, to additional thousands of emails, texts, calls, Facebook posts, voicemail messages, and for food (both physical and spiritual) to nourish our weakened spirits. I am touched beyond ability to put it into words.

We are early on into this journey, but we have already been incredibly blessed in so many ways. Throughout our time together on this site, I will try to enumerate these blessings as they come to mind, although certainly not in order of importance. It is just amazing to see God at work in this and in so many ways, even in the little things, many times through some of you.

So here we are—day one at MD Anderson Cancer Center (MDA). This is blessing number one: just having the good fortune to be treated at this world-class facility. Once you step onto the campus here, you are immediately aware of the fact that they take the eradication of this disease in its many forms very seriously—and, they are good at it. It was reassuring to say the least. At the same time, it revealed blessing number two. A quick look around you and it is readily evident that, as serious as my situation is, there are countless others struggling with far more complex challenges than mine. So in that moment of realization, I paused to consider the blessing of fifty-nine years of great health and to pray that my encounter with cancer would only be what I have chosen to call it, "a temporary inconvenience."

MDA is as awesome as billed. I met with probably a half-dozen members of the team that will administer patient care during my treatment—among them Dr. Jeffrey Myers, head of the department of head and neck cancer, and one of his residents. We will meet with two to three more doctors from other various disciplines tomorrow. Yet to come is an MRI, which could be Friday or Monday. All of this is going on as they are reviewing the results from the tests that were done previously in Memphis. The treatment plan will probably be formulated next week sometime, and then the fun could start the following week. Still just pulling together all of the facts and having them reviewed by the team. Encouraged and impressed—that sums up day one.

Thank you for walking with me today.

CARINGBRIDGE® JOURNAL ENTRY #2
MAY 2, 2015

WALK OR WORKOUT?

When Lesa and I go on an exercise walk, she gets a better workout than I do simply because it takes three steps for her to match my one stride. It's been that way for over forty years now (including the several years that we dated before marrying). That's somewhat like our day two experience at MDA.

I'm walking at the normal pace, but the MDA team is working feverishly to move my case to the next point. They are incredibly organized to the point of frustration at times, but the result is a focused and efficient system that is patient-centric, which we'll have to admit is quite an exception in the healthcare system in general.

The protocol has become real predictable:

1. You check your MDA app on your phone for your appointment schedule for the day. Schedules are real time, so you are subject to appointments being added on the fly throughout the day.

2. Upon arrival, you are *promptly* escorted to an examination room where you are greeted individually by the doctor's

nurse, a resident or intern, and then the doctor (in that order). You get to repeat your life story for each of them. They don't rely on the information that has previously been entered into your record—they want to know from you personally, and if they discover something new that was left out in the previous dozen reenactments, then for them that's a new finding and could be an important one that contributes to your diagnosis and treatment plan.

3. When the doctor arrives on cue after the first two interrogations, they are professional, but each have been uniquely so. They give you their interpretation of the situation, take whatever time to answer your questions, remind you that theirs is only one piece of the puzzle and that the final diagnosis and treatment plan will be decided by the tumor board, which convenes on Thursday of each week. That is where my case, along with the others that they are dealing with, are individually reviewed, and a consensus is reached among the board of fifty physicians.

4. Then we are off to our next stop. Now understand that all of this is done while maintaining a very precise schedule, which truly makes you feel like all of these people are working only on your case and you are their most important patient.

On the one hand, we've been conditioned to expect rapid responses, fact-based decisions, and caregivers that are masters at making you feel both comfortable and confident in their comments and conclusions. But when you encounter someone that doesn't emulate that model, fear and doubt rear their ugly heads. You are quickly reminded that you are a cancer patient with a deadly disease in a very challenging location to remove and/or treat. And then there are test results (biopsy slides) that remain "in transit," holding all of the doctors in limbo as they wait on this critical information to arrive and be further analyzed by their experts.

In the midst of all of this, I was reminded of the first Bible verse that I remember learning. It is Psalms 56:3 and says simply, "When I am afraid, I put my trust in you." Pretty simple for a young child in the beginners' class of a small rural church but totally adequate for a mature adult facing one of my biggest fears.

So, blessing number three: I am reminded of those who took a vested interest in my salvation at an early age, who taught me the importance of God's Word in the practical things in life. I have held on to that verse probably more than any other through the years, although they would teach me many more. So thank you Mrs. Parker, White, O'Neal, Griffin, and others for your impact on my life that transcends time.

And to each of you . . .

Thank you for walking with me today.

CARINGBRIDGE® JOURNAL ENTRY #3
MAY 3, 2015

WALKING WITH FAMILY

D ay three was scheduled to be a day off—not for good behavior but simply because the appropriate next tests could not be scheduled until Monday. Actually, day three was quiet except for the follow-up call from one of the physicians indicating his take on my situation and that he was adding yet another test on Monday to serve as a baseline for future treatment comparisons. My rookie estimation at this point is that we won't know anything "official" regarding treatment until late this coming week, as it will be then before all of the remaining clinicals can be performed, read, interpreted, and applied to the overall diagnosis landscape.

So, I am left with another beautiful day in Houston on which to reflect on the incredible blessings that are coming my way in the midst of all of this conflict. These blessings tend to take one of two forms: a new manifestation or a reminder of something that has been there all along but that I have taken for granted. Blessing number four—my wonderful family—falls into that second group. This week, for the first time in over ten years, I have found myself surrounded exclusively by my loving wife and two wonderful daughters, and it has been a little slice of heaven. Now don't misunderstand me, I love my sons-in-law and my grandchildren immensely, but it afforded me the opportunity to bask in a time in our lives that, well, at least in retrospect, was not as complicated. I'm so thankful that both of the girls were able to join me for the first few days of this walk to provide encouragement, moral support, Daddy hugs, and just a whole lot of lovin'.

Their value has been immeasurable. Lindsay (known to her Daddy as "Biggest" only because she was the first born, and when number two came along, I wanted to instill in her a sense of importance—for her to be the role model for her baby sister) took charge of personally transporting us to our many appointments and flawlessly navigated downtown Houston. As much as I have prided myself in the past of navigating with relative ease, with everything that the patient in me is having to process, I really struggled to familiarize myself with the new terrain. And MDA is not all together in one convenient spot but rather is surrounded by countless other hospitals and clinics and medical offices. Even as organized as *they* are, it can be rather confounding for the first-time patient.

Whitney (aka "Baby Girl," "My Baby," or just "Baby"—so called because, well, she's the baby!) provided insight on the medical aspects. Whenever someone rattled off something that sounded like it came from a third year medical student textbook, we'd turn to Whitney, who would put it into words that our foggy brains could understand. Of course with that knowledge and expertise comes the burden that "hey, you're talking about my Daddy." This weighs heavy on her in spite of the unwavering faith that we all have that God is in control. And for both of the girls, just having them here meant so much. I'm blessed that they both insisted on being here, but at my urging, both went home early to try and maintain a sense of normalcy in their respective households. God has blessed me with two wonderful daughters who have grown into model Christian mothers and wives. My pride for them and of them knows no bounds.

And, of course, I saved the best for last. For almost five years, I called her my girlfriend. For the last thirty-seven years, ten months, and twenty-three days I have proudly called her my wife. She's been my best friend and a model mother to our children, supporter, coach, business partner, and chief counsel . . . and now my 24/7 caregiver. I could not ask for more. She's been beside me in good and not so good. Her faith has been amazingly demonstrated from day one of my diagnosis, and her every action reminds me that defeat is not an option. A quick look at either of our girls and you immediately know they are her daughters—not for just their features but for the grace and love they got from their mother. I am indeed a blessed man.

The journey is far easier with family at your side!

Thank you for walking with me today.

CARINGBRIDGE® JOURNAL ENTRY #4
MAY 5, 2015

WALKING WITH FRIENDS

Never in my life have I felt the magnitude of love and support that has come over the last week since our journey led us to Houston. I shared yesterday of the support from my nuclear family, but it only begins there. My sister, Sharon, my brother, Steve, and a host of cousins have reached out and pledged their support. Many of you back at home in Memphis are wearing bracelets that read "No One Fights Alone," uniting our spirits in my personal fight against this disease. My peers at work are all going the extra mile to cover for me in my absence. Extended family, church family, work family . . . all are part of the blessing of family.

It has amazed me how God continues to put people in our path as a constant reminder of His sovereignty over my health concerns. There was the clinical nurse who boldly assured us that the diagnosis is not the end of the story but rather the opportunity for God to reveal Himself. She then pulled out of the inside pocket of her lab coat a copy of Dodie Osteen's book chronicling her miraculous healing of cancer in 1981 and handed it to me. Then she pressed her business card into Lesa's hand on which she wrote, *When in doubt, call me.* What an exercise of belief in His faithfulness and an opportunity for one of His children to be His hands and His feet in a broken world.

It doesn't end there, but, let me digress a moment. Do you believe in angels? I do . . . but, hang with me here, I'm not talking about the ones in the white flowing robes with the huge floppy wings. I believe in those too, but I am referring to angels who randomly show up at just the right place in God's appointed time to minister to His children. I first knowingly encountered them in 1994. I had just been fired from a high level job that a few years earlier had required me to relocate our young family (kids were in middle school) to Nashville. The disappointment, embarrassment, anger, and uncertainty of the future all had me emotionally paralyzed and holed up in our Brentwood home.

Then, out of the blue and quite unannounced, two friends of ours from our former hometown just showed up on our front doorstep. It didn't take long for my secret to get out, but oh my, how they ministered to both me and my family that weekend.

Now here is where it really gets cool. For probably twenty-one years since that encounter, we have kept in touch with them only through Christmas cards, Facebook, and an occasional text. Their career path has led them from north Georgia, to Russia, to New York City, and then . . . get this . . . to Metro Houston, Texas (Conroe, to be specific). So one of the first calls we got after determining our course of treatment would be at MDA came from Ann and Larry Ray. And just as before, they have offered love and support, just as many of you have. So blessings five and six are strangers who have already touched us with random acts and friends who, just as Larry and Ann, have faithfully kept us in your thoughts and prayers in addition to the incredible other acts of support. We thank God continuously for you.

So day six at MDA was spent in more tests—first a two-hour MRI in the morning followed by another CT scan in the afternoon and a second consultation with one of my physicians. I anticipate knowing the plan of attack by the end of the week. Until then, pray fervently with me for an accurate diagnosis and insight for the team on how best to treat it.

Thank you for walking with me today.

CARINGBRIDGE® JOURNAL ENTRY #5
MAY 7, 2015

WALKING IN FAITH

OK, understand that as much as I would like to, I simply can't reply to every email, text, voicemail, CaringBridge® post, Facebook post, phone call, card, letter, etc., that you have been so kind to send my way. This you can know for sure: if you took the time to do one of the above, I promise you that it has been personally read by me—probably several times. I have attempted to acknowledge each and every one with a "like" where possible, but please do not take offense if I have not replied to you. I have truly appreciated your interest and your willingness to walk with me along a path I have never personally traversed. So I'll try to do my part in keeping you informed if you will help me by graciously responding, as many of you already have. Looking back over the last week, we haven't gone that far, so the real challenges of the journey are still ahead.

With 2,195,914—plus 4—Houston is ranked the most populous city in Texas and the fourth most populous city in the United States. As they have a tendency to do everything BIG in Texas, it was only appropriate that they *all* showed up to welcome the four of us to town last Tuesday—all 2,195,914 of them, it seemed, were in rush hour traffic with us. As we inched along at nano-pace (yes, it is a word—I just made it up last night playing Scrabble) in a sea of seemingly parked vehicles, I marveled at that statistic. I peered into windows of cars, trucks, and eighteen-wheelers, and pulled alongside motorcyclists wondering what each of their stories were. Were many of them, like me, headed to the renowned cancer research center for answers and treatment toward an ultimate cure? The American Cancer Society tells us that one in every four men will die of some form of cancer while for women the odds improve to one in five. But if the statistics are right, then that only accounts for twenty- to twenty-five percent of those thousands of commuters on this busy highway on this sunny Tuesday afternoon. What about the others?

I look into a mini-van, clearly that of a soccer mom, and in the back was her son (in uniform)—the two headed to practice or perhaps a game. Is she a single mom, trying to cover the role of both parents and feeling the pains of a marriage lost and her precious family left reeling in its wake? Or what about the guy driving the big rig that keeps inching by as we each take turns at momentary leads in the seemingly endless procession? He's clearly alone in that rig today as he carries his company's load to the contracted destination. But what about the personal load of regret, torn relationships, and disappointment that he carries every day . . . alone?

It's not the first time that I've had such thoughts. As vast as it is today, Houston is only a microcosm of the world that we call ours. It seems that every time I find myself as one of a huge delegation, whether at a sporting event, in snarled traffic like that of Houston, or in the bustling mega-metropolis of Shanghai, China, my finite mind can't seem to grasp the fact that the very Creator of the universe knows each and every one of them by name; that He knows the number of hairs on their heads and the grains of sand beneath their feet. But more amazing than that is the fact that He takes a personal interest in my life and in yours. In my health and in yours. In my vocation and in yours. In my future and yours. I can't fathom it. It's all about faith.

Tommy Walker wrote a great song that is very simple:

I have a Maker
He formed my heart
Before even time began
My life was in his hands

I have a Father
He calls me His own
He'll never leave me
No matter where I go

[Chorus]
He knows my name
He knows my every thought
He sees each tear that falls
And He hears me when I call [1]

Today has been a really good day. Lesa and I were able to break away from MDA and return to Memphis for a few days before the diagnosis is determined and the treatment plan begins. But as soon as we know more, you'll be hearing from me.

Thank you for walking with me today.

CARINGBRIDGE® JOURNAL ENTRY #6
MAY 9, 2015

WALKING WITH YOUR MOTHER

Happy Mother's Day!
     To all of you who have the distinct pleasure and honor of holding the title of Mom, Mother, Mama, or any other affectionately termed moniker coined by those to whom you have given birth, you are deserving of far more love, admiration, and appreciation than one day a year! It is your dedication, commitment, and unconditional love for your children that will profoundly impact them for the rest of their lives. It is an awesome responsibility and one that both you and they will come to realize more and more with each passing year. So regardless of how botched a job they may do of delighting you with breakfast in bed, or picking out the right card or present, or forgetting to make lunch reservations until the day of . . . just know that there's no way they can truly get it right, for you deserve far more!

     You're probably thinking, *Well that is a nice gesture, but what does this have to do with his journey with cancer?* It has everything to do with it, for you see, I ceased being able to tell my mother, "Happy Mother's Day" after she succumbed to her own five-year battle with breast cancer in 1973. I was thirteen years old when she was diagnosed, and I witnessed firsthand enough of the devastating effects of cancer on an individual and their family to last a lifetime. But those eighteen years we shared had an immense influence on me.

First of all, she blessed me with life. My mom had just turned forty the month before I was born, and in 1955, giving birth at that age was a risky proposition both for the mother and child. My older brother and sister often lovingly referred to me as "the accident," although it took me years to figure out what they meant by that. Times were hard . . . yet, she chose life. For her, any other option was probably never a consideration.

Second, she blessed me by modeling the perfect example of biblical motherhood through both instruction and action. During one Sunday evening church service, at the time for the altar call, the pastor had made a particular appeal to the women in attendance, and the ladies of our small Baptist congregation were lined up in the front from wall to wall. Before the invitation concluded, I slipped out of my seat and joined my mother down front. When the pastor asked me why I had come, I replied, "Well, I am not real sure, but I know that if my mother needs to be down here, then I surely do."

Third, she blessed others with a bold Christian witness. She truly cared about the spiritual condition of those she encountered at church, at work, and throughout the community. For years after her death, people would come up to me and share about the impact she'd made on their lives either at work or even during one of her many hospital stays. Regarding the reason she had to bear the disease, she said to never ask, "Why?" From her, I learned the grace by which she faced one day at a time with hope and faith in an unwavering and all-sufficient God.

She set the example of *how to make the journey make a difference.* My prayer is that I may do the same.

Thank you for walking with me today.

CARINGBRIDGE® JOURNAL ENTRY #7
MAY 12, 2015

WALKING ... OUT OF CONTROL

It's Monday, it's raining, and the Grammy-award-winning Carpenters' tune is on perpetual repeat mode in my head. Our journey this morning leads us back to Houston, and our new "home away from home" is only 598 miles in front of our car. The GPS says nine hours and fourteen minutes. Clearly whoever designs this mapping software is too young to appreciate the curse of frequent urination or the need to have "fork food" instead of fast food, not to mention the desire to stretch your legs at least every couple of hours. Unlike the lyrics of that 70s tune, I refuse to let "rainy days and Mondays get me down."

However, as the Memphis skyline slowly disappears in the rearview mirror, the low-grade headaches that have come to be a more frequent companion have returned. Is it the gray and gloomy band of thunderstorms that clearly paint themselves on the western sky and define the front that is about to bring copious rain and perhaps damaging winds to the next ten-plus hours of driving? Is it the stress of this coupled with the anticipation of my next consult with the surgeon and team lead on Wednesday? Karen Carpenter, move over—I need to write these questions down while I am thinking of them; I need to prepare myself for whatever the next round of dialogue may present, what those next steps may be, and how soon we can get with the program. Those of you who have traveled interstate I-40 between Memphis and Texarkana know what a boring drive that can be, particularly on an early Monday morning when truck traffic seems to be slow in waking up. So you have a lot of time to think.

Now I am a self-proclaimed control freak, readily attested by those who know and love me and readily tolerated by those who work with me. I also am the first to say that I have gotten better about "letting go" over the last few years, although there still remains doubt among the aforementioned parties. Part of this is a result of the stark realization that I am uniquely not in control of this immediate health situation. Like most of us, I feel the need to try and fix things on my own.

While I have a lot of scripture that are favorites, the wise words of Solomon have always inspired me. Proverbs 3:5-6 reminds us to "Trust in the Lord with all your heart and lean not on your own understanding; in all your ways submit to him, and he will make your paths straight." But it took yet another blessing for me to make that a verse of focus rather than one of convenience.

The car came from seemingly nowhere. I was in the hammer lane, trying to avoid the numerous craters and potholes that this past winter's snow and ice had left in need of repair in the more traveled right lane. It was a small Nissan sedan, older but not that old. It was a goldish-brown color, and positioned on the trunk deck were two Arkansas Razorback Hog decals facing each other (I know, God help them). And this car was passing me on the right. But it wasn't all of the above that caught my attention. It was the message that was intended for me this Monday morning as my head pounded with self-induced doubt. There, in clear unobstructed view, positioned in the center of the rear glass, was a window graphic that read, *God is in control.*

Now, for those of you who do not know, I make my living in the sale of auto accessories. I've made it my business over the last twenty years to know my product categories very well—both the product offering of my vendors and those of my competitors. I have never seen that graphic. Perhaps it was customized for the owner of the Nissan. My take is that they may have liked it and bought it, but the message was clearly mine today.

As the vehicle continued to pull away in the distance, I was impressed by the fact that he or she had passed me on the right, enabling me to have full visibility of the words. If our lane position had been reversed, and the car had passed on the driver's side, the A-pillar in the minivan (the post that frames the windshield from the hood of the car to the roof) would have most likely obstructed my view, or I would not have paid attention to the vehicle that was passing in the more conventional fashion.

My schedule on Wednesday resumes at MDA with seven appointments over the next two days, culminating on Thursday at 2:00 p.m. with a second biopsy. This one will be CT guided, so as always, I covet your prayers as we approach these critical tests and consults. Because we know who is in control.

Thank you for walking with me today.

CARINGBRIDGE® JOURNAL ENTRY #8
MAY 14, 2015

WALKING IN A MARATHON

W ell, my week (at least for now) has come to an end at MDA. But schedules are always subject to change, and I am readily available at their beck and call. After seven appointments in two days, I celebrated the last of the seven this evening after a successful five-hour (from start to finish) CT-guided biopsy. They were successful in a number of respects: not only were they able to obtain a total of ten samples of critical evidence that should hold the keys to an accurate diagnosis, they did so without doing any apparent *collateral damage*. That's my term for all of the things that could go wrong in that procedure, particularly because the area of concern has so many critical nerves, vessels, and structures. It's a scary list of things that could go wrong—the virtual "fine print" that so many of us prefer to just skip over and sign the release in desperation to get the answers that are needed.

Knowing that we were apprehensive, we thank God for the many answered prayers that were voiced today at and around 2:00 p.m. as my actual procedure began. Not only did we experience confidence and peace, we were once again reassured that the second biopsy was needed, and we were in the hands of a very experienced team. So today was an important milestone and additional evidence of answered prayer.

Many of you know that I am a distance runner. It has become my way of squeezing exercise into a very busy schedule. My event of choice is the half marathon (13.1 miles) even though I have finished one full marathon of 26.2 miles. But as much as I enjoy the sub-two-hour participation in the organized events, the real work is put into logging many, many more miles and hours than that over weeks and months in preparation for the big day of the race.

This journey is very similar to a marathon. We just completed day sixteen since our first day at MDA, and at this point, we know very little more than when we arrived. That is somewhat hard to accept, but we are very early into this race. But like marathon training, you gain strength and endurance from every time you get out there. The first few times you begin working in anticipation of an upcoming race, it's a struggle to get in the first few miles. Then, you reach a point where you clear that physical hurdle and are able to "comfortably" run a longer distance, where your body accepts the punishment you are putting it through. Breathing becomes regulated, muscle tone improves, endurance grows, and it can even become . . . well, enjoyable. Once you reach that point (and it takes determination and work), the miles can be added on at a much faster rate, and you really begin to see and feel progress.

But I would be lying if I told you that marathon training is a pleasant experience, particularly if you have never been a runner. You face physical pain, emotional uncertainty, doubt, and desperation at some point or even at multiple points in the journey. You have to push through those times because, believe me, the finish is worth it all.

It's been my experience that training is much easier if you have a running partner. Not only can it cure the monotony of lonely runs by yourself, but you have someone who is depending on you to be there—hot or cold, rainy or clear, sore or in great physical shape, emotionally struggling or feeling content.

I'm confident that we are partnered with absolute world-class trainers and coaches at MDA. You are doing your part by cheering us on, manning the water and first aid stations, and running alongside us (even if for just a few steps). I have found that in running marathons, it's not *where* you finish but *that* you finish. That's why we've chosen to walk this marathon and are so blessed that you have chosen to join us.

Thank you for walking with me today.

CARINGBRIDGE® JOURNAL ENTRY #9
MAY 19, 2015

WALKING IN PLACE

More *hurry up—and wait.* Just when I thought my patience was improving, in His providence, God has gently reminded me once again that I am not in control. We are awaiting the interpretation of last week's biopsy and from there (hopefully), a clear direction for a treatment plan and the timing of such. In many ways, the waiting is the most difficult part. At least that is what those who have walked this path before have repeatedly told me of their experiences.

Last Wednesday, as we met with Dr. Myers, he clarified the need for the second biopsy. As I asked him what caused doubt in their minds with the original findings sent from Memphis, he rolled his chair over to the desk to pull up my MRI images taken the week before. All of the other imaging reports that had been shared with me may have been easily interpreted by the specialists in the room, but for me, it was just different looks at the same abstract painting of grays and blacks. I could make out the outline of my head, but from that point on, I have to admit I was lost.

But this MRI image was different. My alleged nemesis was staring back at me from the computer monitor with vivid detail. What shocked me was the mass—not its presence but its size. From the original diagnosis, the reference points were stated in centimeters (no wonder I was surprised—another reason we should have abandoned the metric system when we had the chance!). The surgeon patiently walked us through the orientation of the various perspectives, explaining that the image on the screen was as if viewing my head from the front and lying on my back. He pointed out the differences in the ear canal, which was compressed on the left (reinforcing the hearing issues that were the early signs of my problem). The triangular boundaries of the parapharyngeal space were fully occupied on the left side—a stark contrast from a "normal" representation on the right. The protrusions from the left side of my jaw that have caused difficulty in eating and from the soft pallet that partially restricts my airway were clearly evident. He explained that the additional biopsy would either confirm the earlier findings or add clarity to other potential avenues for effective treatment.

Sorry, when you signed up to accompany me on this journey, I should have had you sign a disclosure stating that you understood you were in it for the duration—for good news or bad news, ugly details or pretty ones. You're probably thinking the above specifics were better left unsaid. Well, I learned early on that one of the first keys to success at MDA is open communication, so I will do the same with you.

But fear not! That's not just my command, it comes from the Bible and is the most repeated command found there. Don't you find it odd that God chose those words to be scattered strategically and repeatedly time and time again throughout His instruction manual for mankind? Of course, He knew that we would need the constant reminders—particularly the control freaks like you and me.

As my frustration with the continued delays were beginning to noticeably surface over the last few days, my daughter Lindsay sent me the following poem written by J. D. Smith, which served as a very timely additional reminder:

Waiting! Yes, patiently waiting!
Till next steps made plain shall be;
To hear, with the inner hearing,
The Voice that will call for me.

Waiting! Yes, hopefully waiting!
With hope that need not grow dim;
The Master is pledged to guide me,
And my eyes are unto Him.

Waiting! Expectantly waiting!
Perhaps it may be today
The Master will quickly open
The gate to my future way.

Waiting! Yes, waiting! still waiting!
I know, though I've waited long,
That, while He withholds His purpose,
His waiting cannot be wrong.

Waiting! Yes, waiting! still waiting!
The Master will not be late:
He knoweth that I am waiting
For Him to unlatch the gate. [2]

As the past week of our journey has been spent on the conditioning track running mindless repetitions, the countless circles don't seem to be moving us any closer to our destination. But they are preparing us for the race that lies ahead. Don't attempt to run the race without that critical preparation. Are you ready?

Thank you for walking with me today.

---

2.   Taken from *Streams In The Desert* by L.B. Cowman Copyright © 2006 by L.B. Cowman. Used with permission of Zondervan. www.zondervan.com.

CARINGBRIDGE® JOURNAL ENTRY #10
MAY 20, 2015

WALKING IN THE POWER OF WORDS

T he text came out of the blue. It wasn't the fact *that* it came or *from whom* it came but *when* it came that got my attention. It was day one at MDA, the first appointment with the renowned surgeon who had agreed to take my case at the request of an esteemed colleague back in Memphis. The family had just been called back to the exam room for our initial consult, and as I lowered myself into my chair, the vibrating text prompt went off on my phone in the back pocket of my jeans. It was as if it were screaming out, *Hey, don't sit on me!* Normally I would have quieted it and viewed the text later, but the prompt just seemed to have a sense of urgency about it. And, well, I have a whole new sensitivity to *urgent* these days.

The time signature indicated that it came in at 10:48 a.m. It was from a business contact, but very early into the commentary she diverted from discussions of business to my more pressing personal health issues. Her words spoke of her observations of my faith in God, and she pledged to continue to pray for me and my family. It was so special.

In many ways it was not that different from the scores of other communications that I and my family have received over the last twenty-three days. What made it truly exceptional was *when* I got it. God used those words of encouragement and affirmation to bless me that morning at exactly the time I needed it most. It was as if He was saying, *See, you are making a difference.* His timing is truly extraordinary, and this was just another example of it.

Our words are so powerful—both for good to build up and for evil to destroy. We've all said things in the past that we wish we could take back, but if you are like me, you have missed far more opportunities to lift up and offer words of affirmation and encouragement. How many times have I kicked myself for not seizing those opportunities! What about you? Is there someone that you have been meaning to reach out to . . . to give support, rectify a misunderstanding, affirm an act, or perhaps restore a relationship? Never delay saying what you want to say. Your words can have great meaning, and they may be used by God at just the right time—as I am convinced that text was on day one at MDA.

So many of you have kindly commented on my CaringBridge® journal entries since we began our walk together. Those uplifting words and the encouragement have meant so much. Forgive me that I have not been faithful to respond, but understand that each time you enter guestbook messages, I see and appreciate them all. It's my way of staying connected with the people that mean so much to me.

Thank you for walking with me today.

WALKING IN A STORM

If you have been watching the news at all over the last couple of weeks, you have no doubt seen numerous references to the exceptionally heavy rainfall that the state of Texas has experienced. After several weeks of copious daily doses, meteorologists have officially declared an end to the drought that has been plaguing them for the last five years, as it seems that all of that pent-up rainfall has attempted to dump at one time onto a very saturated surface. So as chance would have it, we found ourselves, on Memorial Day, driving in a Texas-sized deluge so intense that Mark Wiggins diverted from the interstate roadway to seek safe shelter (and fuel) to ride out the storm. Those who have traveled with me know that few things can stop me from my intended destination once we are underway. So this stop alone was an unexpected turn.

After an hour or more of sitting along with other motorists cramped under the confines of the Exxon fuel center canopy, I was finally able to maneuver into position to refuel, and we were once again on our way. The powerful storm was beginning to break up, and the western horizon revealed the very clear trailing edge of the dark band of thunderstorms. It was as if a black window shade had been pulled down all the way, except for enough to peak underneath to reveal what could be best described as the dawning of a new day. At first it appeared as an inch-wide band of golden light spread evenly along the margin of the shade. The further we drove into the storm, we began to see the evidence that it would soon be over, as that narrow band on the horizon expanded more and more.

Then, suddenly, as if on cue, the setting sun continued its downward path, and its rays burst forth from the cloud bank out from under the "shade." In our mirrors, the dissipating clouds behind us reflected a tapestry of pinks and mauves, and what had previously been a wicked storm was miraculously turned into a thing of sheer beauty. We marveled at the lightshow in front of us as we shielded our eyes from the brilliance ahead but were awestruck by the beauty that was now left behind us. We struggled repeatedly to capture it with our cameras but failed to get a true representation of what we just witnessed.

This journey that we are on has already taken a number of unexpected turns. Yet, if I take the time to listen and look, I can see God at work all around me. First of all—that we have been safe from all of the inclement weather, while in our "home away from home" or on the road, traveling. But far more evident is His work in my own personal storm. I'm reminded to keep my eyes clearly fixed on the Light on the horizon and not on the dark clouds immediately overhead. I pray that He will turn this storm of mine into a thing of beauty.

Yesterday was another one of those encounters, as I found myself back at MDA for another CT scan. It was uneventful. After more blood work, I met with Dr. Myers, who again shared with me that we are still awaiting the additional biopsy tests that had been ordered due to the continued uncertainty of the specific type of tumor as well as its malignancy potential. Part of this, no doubt, is due to a holiday weekend combined with an epic flood of the Houston area, limiting travel to and from work at MDA. Or could it be that the difficulty in determining what would otherwise be a routine diagnosis is God's way of bringing His purpose to fruition? I arrived in Houston over a month ago with what was believed to be a clear diagnosis of a specific type of cancer that had already been determined to be malignant (and it may well be). But that diagnosis has pretty well been ruled out, and the malignancy potential continues to be uncertain. Yes . . . another unexpected turn in the road.

What has been determined, however, is that surgery will be a necessary part and the beginning point of our treatment. The date has still not been determined, as it will require a minimum of three surgeons of varying disciplines to be involved. As one of them said, "It will be a big deal." So we continue to wait with our eyes fixed on the horizon of hope, taking refuge in the only One who masters all storms.

> *God is our refuge and strength, an ever-present help in trouble. (Psalm 46:1)*
>
> *Keep me safe, my God, for in you I take refuge. (Psalm 16:1)*
>
> *You evildoers frustrate the plans of the poor, but the Lord is their refuge. (Psalm 14:6)*
>
> *In the fear of Jehovah is strong confidence; And his children shall have a place of refuge. (Proverbs 14:26 ASV)*
>
> *Be merciful to me, O God, be merciful to me, for in you my soul takes refuge; in the shadow of your wings I will take refuge, till the storms of destruction pass by. (Psalm 57:1 ESV)*

Thank you for walking with me today.

CARINGBRIDGE® JOURNAL ENTRY #12
JUNE 5, 2015

WALKING IN HIS FAITHFULNESS

Some days clearly stand out as waypoints for life's journey. You know, the ones that somehow mark defining moments that are indelibly etched into your life's story, without which none of us would know or appreciate adversity, trials, or utter despondency. I'm not talking about one of those, "Where were you when Kennedy was assassinated?" incidents, or in the case of you kids, "Where were you when you got the news that Michael Jackson had died?" I'm talking about a truly up close and personal, defining moment.

I celebrated the anniversary of one of those days for the twenty-first time last week: May 31, 1994. It was a day that began much like today—beautifully sunny with summer's heat just beginning to make its presence known. Little did I know that before that day's end, I would be faced with one of the greatest challenges of my life. Just when everything appeared to be headed in the right direction, life threw me a curve ball. By 5:00 p.m., I had been fired!

How do you explain to your wife that leaving your dream home (that had just been built) for the "opportunity to lead the merger of two nationwide companies" had apparently been a bad decision? How do you tell your middle-school-aged children—who you have just less than three years earlier uprooted from every constant they had ever known and moved them eight hours to begin a new and better life—that they may get to do it all over again?

For the first time in my life, I was unemployed and emotionally and fiscally unprepared to face what was staring me square in the face: a mortgage with little equity, relocation costs (again), college educations (two of them at out-of-state rates = six of them), weddings, etc.

But life's journey will teach us lessons if we pause long enough to notice them. It took that career crash landing for me to realize that I was not really in control but that God had a *better* way when there seemed to be *no* way. Through it surfaced the clear understanding that a marriage founded in a common faith will endure such tests. Lesa, your belief in me and commitment to our marriage was a constant inspiration and kept me going when I had doubts that the dark clouds that followed me overhead would ever clear again. Your willingness to do whatever was necessary to keep us afloat during those first few years while maintaining a stable household is a testament to that commitment. (I still can't believe I allowed you to do those jobs—we weren't that desperate, were we?)

I also learned that kids grounded in that same faith are incredibly resilient and will learn from and rise above that adversity when they, as their parents, heed the call to God's leading. Lindsay and Whitney, thanks for making the personal sacrifices to allow us to walk through that open door almost twenty-one years ago. You never once complained, and I realize that our nomadic journey must have been incredibly difficult at times for both of you. If I appeared insensitive to that, please forgive me.

There's no doubt that the twenty-one years of abundant blessings that came from that fork in my career path gives a perspective that knows no bounds. I wish I could say that I knew the way this story was going to turn out twenty-one years ago. I believed it would all work out, but I will have to be honest and tell you that my faith said, "yes," but my sight said, "it's a long shot." God's hand has been on us from the start, and I know that He will be faithful to complete the work He has started in us.

There's a tattered card that remains in my wallet after twenty-one years of abuse. The anniversary of when I first received it is coming up in a few days. It has outlived several wallets, sustained sweat, unexpected dips in the lake, and constant weathering of bills and receipts rubbing against it as they lingered there awhile before moving on far too quickly. It's at the center of the wallet, positioned there as a reminder to help keep me "centered." There was writing once on the back, penned in ink that has long since faded away. It said, "Daddy, I've been wanting to give you this for a while . . . I thought now would be a good time!" It was a good time then, and it has been for twenty-one years and will hopefully be for many more to come. The printed side says simply, *Lord, help me remember that nothing is going to happen to me today that You and I together can't handle.*

So this is not the first time I've encountered His unending faithfulness in my life. Volumes could not contain my meager attempts at recounting them all. But I have grown to look forward to that date in May each year as a reminder of an earlier time in my life when God rescued me from the certain depths of despair. And while I was devastated and confused, He provided direction and assurance. In retrospect, I'm almost of the opinion that everyone should have to walk through the fire of unemployment once in their life to gain an appreciation for what they have and a dependence on God to lead them down the right path at those critical junctures.

Although it's been a week since our last update, there has been little to report. However, we do have a date set for surgery—July 2—and I plan on celebrating my "independence" from the tumor at MDA while you guys celebrate yours at the lake, or by the pool, or simply with family and friends. We do have so much to be thankful for. As we know more, I will be sharing accordingly.

Thanks for your steadfast love, concern, support, and most of all, your prayers! Continue to pray for a clear diagnosis, that the tumor will be benign, that its growth will be arrested and even reversed, and for the vast team that will be involved in the upcoming surgery.

> *Now faith is the assurance of things hoped for, the conviction of things not seen. (Hebrews 11:1 ESV)*

> *Your love, Lord, reaches to the heavens, your faithfulness to the skies. (Psalm 36:5)*

Thank you for walking with me today!

CARINGBRIDGE® JOURNAL ENTRY #13
JUNE 15, 2015

WALKING IN HIS PROTECTION

Today is immunization shot day for Mary Collins Tolbert, granddaughter number one and the second grandchild of our flock of four. While she's almost five years old and pretty smart, she has no idea of the day that lies in store for her. But her loving parents know that those shots will prevent her from far worse maladies than the temporary pain and soreness at the injection sites. I'm sure that if they clearly explained the pain and the uncertainty the day would bring for her, then, even in her own limited understanding and frailty, she would say, *Thanks, but no thanks.*

Isn't that a lot like our lives as adults? Sometimes our paths lead us to situations where, in our own limited understanding of the path before us, we'd rather opt out. Yet in His infinite wisdom, our heavenly Father knows what is in store for us and that what may seem at the time to be painful and unfair is only a part of our own "growing up."

The latest news from MDA last week is that biopsy number two's results are not a lot more conclusive than the first. The additional stains and molecular tests of those needle biopsies that were requested only ruled out additional suspect varieties—so, we are learning more about what it is not but still have no confirmation of what it is, and its malignancy potential is "uncertain." The upcoming surgery on July 2 will hopefully provide adequate tissue samples to answer these key questions. Until then, we'll keep on walking.

> *"For I know the plans I have for you," declares the Lord, "plans to prosper you and not to harm you, plans to give you hope and a future." (Jeremiah 29:11)*

Thank you for walking with me today!

CARINGBRIDGE® JOURNAL ENTRY #14
JUNE 17, 2015

WALKING IN THE DARK

My cousin Bill is the definition of a practical jokester. He, along with his older brother, Raley (aka Pete), lived with my aunt and uncle no more than one hundred fifty yards down the road from our house. I say, "down the road" because it was just that—down in both distance and elevation. They had a fishpond, and my earliest training in patience was spent on its banks waiting for a prized catch.

As Bill was over ten years my elder, we didn't have a lot in common, but he loved to pick on me because I was next to youngest of the fourteen grandkids, and, well, I was an easy target to make fun of. With my disproportionate ears and emaciated frame, I was often referred to as the poster child for those "Project Hope" or "Feed the Children" ads you'd see on your black and white TVs in those days. That, and because I was taught my elders did not lie, I was as gullible as I was a runt.

This morning, as I glanced down at the scar on my right knee that is still clearly visible over fifty years later, I thought back to the incident that caused it that hot summer night in the early 60s.

It was not uncommon for the sun to set on me while fishing at Aunt Sally's pond. Neither was it an exception to be found at their house day or night because I was the courier between her house and ours. But the fact was, it was now dark . . . really dark—there were no streetlights, and I was one hundred fifty yards from the security and safety of my house.

Bill started his routine. "Mama, did they catch those escaped convicts from the county jail? You know, the ones that killed those two little boys?"

Aunt Sally tried unsuccessfully to shame him, but he was already into the monologue.

"They found the smallest boy . . . at least what was left of him after being chopped up by that one convict with the axe."

Now there were few things to be scared of in my little world back then other than the Communists firing a "big one" over from Cuba, and I was really too young to comprehend much of that. But an escaped convict? Now that had my attention. And Bill knew just the buttons to push—and his timing and delivery, a fine science.

As I prepared for my journey home, he said, "Here, Mark, let me turn on the floodlights for you." And of course, I took the bait.

While of some help, the floodlights barely made it to the perimeter of their yard. Peering into the darkness, I found my reference point in the distance. Looking down the terrain that I had traversed back and forth hundreds of times, the porch light at our house across the road and up the hill was on. It yielded far less candlepower than the floods, but it was my beacon of hope, and inside was the security and protection that I was really needing at that moment.

"Go ahead, Mark, I'll keep a watch out for you. I know you are fast . . . but there *are* a couple of them," Bill warned.

Needing no further encouragement and wanting to get as far away from his continued descriptions of the convicts as I could, I leapt onto the path. Years before I would take geometry, I'd already proven that the shortest distance between two points was a straight line, and I was on it. I was about halfway into the area covered by the floodlights when everything went black. Bill had killed the switch, and I was enveloped in a sea of darkness.

In a fraction of a moment (and while continuing to build speed), I assessed my options. *First of all, keep moving,* I thought. *I could circle back in fear and face Bill and Aunt Sally with shame and embarrassment, or I could forge ahead and take my odds that the escaped convicts had not singled me out as their next victim.* I chose the second option.

After reconfirming my bearings by fixing my eyes on the porch light ahead, and with Bill's laughter fading into the background, my skinny legs were just about to hit Mach one. I was halfway now, and I could see the porch light ahead growing brighter. Just one glimpse back over my shoulder to confirm that they were not on my trail when suddenly I was propelled airborne out of control into a full 360-degree flip. My round-off fell short, and I landed firmly on my bottom—just feet away from the road. Dazed but somehow certain that I had now encountered the escapees, one of which must have blindsided me in the dark, I scrambled to my feet and headed across the road to my yard . . . my home . . . my porch light.

It was in the faint glow of that porch light that the true toll of my battle that night was revealed. The price for my fear was a busted knee that later required five stiches. My encounter with convicts was actually a freak but very precise hit with my knee of a highway department grading stake which had been placed only feet to the side of my normal path and driven to the perfect height of a six-year-old's kneecap.

Our imaginations run wild, causing us to fight battles that never exist in the first place. If I had only kept my eyes on the light that night and ran my best (even walked my best), I would have arrived whole, unharmed, and even more confident and prepared for the next time.

We have a Light that leads us through the darkest nights, through the battles we were never intended to fight alone, to claim victories we have never even imagined. May we never lose our focus!

The people walking in darkness have seen a great light; on those living in the land of deep darkness a light has dawned. (Isaiah 9:2)

For God, who said, "Let light shine out of darkness," made his light shine in our hearts to give us the light of the knowledge of God's glory displayed in the face of Christ. (2 Corinthians 4:6)

In him was life, and that life was the light of all mankind. The light shines in the darkness, and the darkness has not overcome it. (John 1:4-5)

Thank you for walking with me today!

CARINGBRIDGE® JOURNAL ENTRY #15
JUNE 25, 2015

WALKING WITH CONFIDENCE

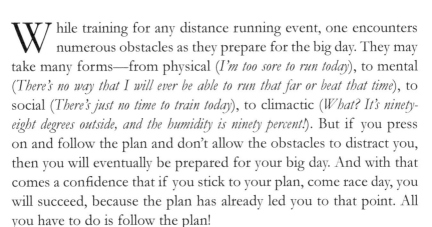

While training for any distance running event, one encounters numerous obstacles as they prepare for the big day. They may take many forms—from physical (*I'm too sore to run today*), to mental (*There's no way that I will ever be able to run that far or beat that time*), to social (*There's just no time to train today*), to climactic (*What? It's ninety-eight degrees outside, and the humidity is ninety percent!*). But if you press on and follow the plan and don't allow the obstacles to distract you, then you will eventually be prepared for your big day. And with that comes a confidence that if you stick to your plan, come race day, you will succeed, because the plan has already led you to that point. All you have to do is follow the plan!

One of our favorite family stories is of Whitney's participation in the Hershey Track and Field games of 1988. Since 1977, the candy maker has sponsored local, district, state, and national competitions for school kids seven to eighteen years of age. So one day, Whitney came home from her second-grade class (of which she was probably the youngest), telling us that she was running in the Hershey's track meet and it was in two weeks.

"The event?" I asked.

"The four hundred meters!" she proudly proclaimed. "Isn't that what you ran, Daddy?"

Well, yes and no. After football season we had the choice of running track or wrestling. So I took the lesser of the two evils. But due to my blinding speed, I never ran competitively in an event. Besides, it was the 440 back then . . . when things were measured in standard units and not metric.

On the following Saturday, we went to the high school stadium to scope out what she'd signed up for. To an eight-year-old, just being on the track in that setting was an enormous shock to her young psyche. Add the competition, the crowd, and the excitement of participation, and you can imagine what would be going on in her young head come race day.

I showed her where her event would start and explained that four hundred meters is a full lap around the track (one-fourth of one mile). "Whitney, if you are going to win this race, you are going to have to run with your *head* and not with your *heart*," I said.

Puzzled, she looked up at me and said, "Uh, I thought you ran with your legs."

"OK, let me break this down a bit," I said. "When the starting gun fires, everyone is going to tear out in a sprint—that is, everyone but you. Your first obstacle will be resisting that temptation to run with the crowd, but believe me, they will burn out, and you will prevail if you run with your head. And that means to start really slow."

From there we walked around to the first turn in the track. I explained that at this point, the others will be far ahead of her, but not until she passed the goal posts could she turn up the speed just a little bit—not a lot, just a little. Walking on to the next quarter behind the opposing team's bleachers, I showed her that at this point in the race, she and the others would be totally blocked from the sight of the fans and everyone cheering them on. It's during this one hundred yards when she would be on her own and would first begin to see the benefits of running the race with her head and not with what her heart was telling her to do. At this point she was instructed to turn up the gas a little more as she began to see the competition running low on fuel and dropping back.

Walking on to the final turn, I instructed her that it was only when she cleared the turn and reached the final stretch could she then give it the remaining gas of all she had left through the finish line. I told her to continue running her race and to not look to either side or behind her but to focus her eyes on the finish line and give it all she's got.

Over the next couple of weeks, we did practice runs, and I tried to instill the plan into her excited little head in just a very limited number of sessions.

Finally the big day of the Hershey meet was here. Hundreds of kids filled the stadium, all longing to see who could run the fastest, jump the highest, or throw the farthest. They called for the girls' seven and under age group for the four hundred meter run. Perhaps six or seven lanes had a participant, and Whitney (clearly the runt of the field) was easy to spot in lane three, sandwiched between two muscular athletes that looked like they had both just signed sponsorships with Nike. *I mean, does anyone check IDs anymore? These kids were clearly over seven years old regardless of how many times they had repeated second grade, and they were built like race horses!* Whitney barely reached their shoulders but was dressed for success in purple shorts, a white top, and matching purple bow. *Well, maybe they will give an award for best dressed*, I thought.

Just as I was beginning to regret having set her up for disappointment, they called the runners to the starting line. The gun fired, and, just as predicted, the field blasted off. Whitney included . . . for about three paces. Then, it was as if something clicked, and "the little machine that could" downshifted into a lope that appeared to be almost in slow motion. Coming out of the first turn, the others were screaming ahead, and as if on cue, you could see Whitney's pace suddenly quicken—maybe not to the crowd, but to her dad. Our friends in the stands were beginning to console us. "What an endeavor for such a little girl," they said.

They entered the blackout period when the field was entirely hidden by the bleachers across the stadium. It didn't take much work to figure out where my daughter was—clearly in last place with half the race remaining. I only hoped that she'd remember to dial up on cues two, three, and four.

As the first runners began to reappear, it was becoming evident that they were beginning to struggle. Wait, there were six runners ahead of Whitney going into the blackout, but now there were only three, and the purple flash hit third gear precisely as instructed. You could see it in her gait—she was clearly a believer now, and the plan was going to work! The second and third place runners were clearly gassed as she blew by them in turn three.

I was amazed as she passed the last of the runners before hitting the stretch and that she still had something left, although that last burst of energy was all she had—both head and heart! All the way through the finish line, the lead continued to build . . . it was legendary! Other events had stopped to witness the incredible finish. The crowds were going wild. You would have thought it was the final heat of the four hundred meters in the Olympic games. First place and a trip to the district finals was hers. We'd just witnessed a miracle—or was it just part of her father's plan?

There were several truths that surfaced for me that day, both as father and coach and as participant of my own race in life. It's times like these that make them seem fresh, although I wish that I had applied them consistently over the years. Here are a few:

1. Don't be deceived by the giant in the lane next to you. He or she may have never even had a plan, much less a coach who controls the outcome of the race.

    Why should I fear when evil days come, when wicked deceivers surround me— (Psalm 49:5)

2. Just run your race. You can't control what is going on in the other lanes. Besides, your plan was designed for you by an omniscient Coach who knows your every strength and weakness.

    I run in the path of your commands, for you have broadened my understanding. (Psalm 119:32)

3. Stay focused on the finish regardless of how bleak things look early on. They never give out trophies for who's leading going into the first turn.

   Do you not know that in a race all the runners run, but only one gets the prize? Run in such a way as to get the prize. (1 Corinthians 9:24)

4. Stay true to your commitment, even though the odds seem overwhelming.

   I instruct you in the way of wisdom and lead you along straight paths. When you walk, your steps will not be hampered; when you run, you will not stumble. (Proverbs 4:11-12)

5. It's OK to fall—just make sure to get back up and stay in the race. The pain of falling can't begin to compare with that of giving up.

   Let perseverance finish its work so that you may be mature and complete, not lacking anything. (James 1:4)

We're one week out from my biggest race ever. I don't know what my life will look like on the other side of this surgery, nor can I begin to comprehend just how sweet a victory celebration over this fierce competitor it will be. But I do know that I have the best Coach with a plan for me that ensures success. His name is Jesus, and there's plenty of room on His training team. May I be faithful to run the course that He has prepared for me, and my prayer today is the same for you!

Thanks for walking with me today!

CARINGBRIDGE® JOURNAL ENTRY #16
JUNE 30, 2015

WALKING WITH THE TEAM

I t's true that an idle mind is the devil's workshop. Throughout this journey, I have found that both the physical and emotional pain can be best managed by staying busy or otherwise focusing on a productive activity and not allowing my mind to shift into idle.

Then again, others in my family have perfected their own remedy, which has been collectively coined as, "stress shopping." No, I didn't say *dress* shopping, although I am told that stress shopping could include but is definitely not limited to dresses. It must be highly effective, because the three women in my life are becoming masters at it. They say, "It is highly therapeutic!" But you know, I think it is great. Charge on, ladies (no, not literally *charge* on). I think either way, I will pay for this paragraph!

Countless numbers of you have so faithfully prayed for me and my family as we face my upcoming surgery this Thursday. It will be the most significant day in our journey this far. So I'd like to implore you to widen the focus of your prayers this week to include our entire medical team. While I don't have all of the participants, each of which will play critical roles, the following are the lead specialists that are lined up to participate in this massive operation that is estimated to last between ten and twelve hours:

- Dr. Jeffrey Myers: Lead Surgeon

- Dr. Paul Gidley: ENT-Otolaryngologist and Oral Surgeon

- Dr. Peirong Yu: Plastic Surgeon

- Dr. Franco DeMonte: Neurosurgeon

Wednesday will be filled with pre-surgery meetings, consults, and further preparation. Then, I'll report to MDA on Thursday morning at 5:00 a.m. for prep, and I'm told they will take me back between 7:00 and 7:30 a.m. and that the procedure will actually begin between 8:00 and 8:15 a.m. (*Lord, I hope somebody remembers to order the pizza and Dr. Pepper for my team!*)

So, until I can sit up with my laptop and a clear head to resume chronicling the journey, I will entrust reports of my progress on CaringBridge® to the three women in my life. After all, this story is theirs as well.

Thanks for hanging with me through your prayers, love, and support over these last few months. We've trained hard together, and the endurance phase of our marathon now begins. There will be days when you will lack the desire or question why you signed up for this, when the doubt will creep in and you just don't feel like you can go on. That's normal, and it would be far easier just to throw in the towel—except you are not running the race alone, and your training partner is counting on you. Press on, never give in, never give up!

Brothers and sisters, I do not consider myself yet to have taken hold of it. But one thing I do: Forgetting what is behind and straining toward what is ahead, I press on toward the goal to win the prize for which God has called me heavenward in Christ Jesus. (Philippians 3:13-14)

Thanks for walking with me today!

***

The day of surgery was finally here. I think in many ways that I was actually looking forward to it. I was ready for relief. I was ready to move forward after months of being poked, prodded, tested, analyzed, and biopsied. My friend Randy McKinney had come in early to be there for the operation. In fact, he treated us to a Houston Astros ballgame the night before. It was a really fun time in a great venue and helped to take our minds off of what was coming up the next day. His wife, Betsy, would be joining us at the hospital later, along with my brother, Steve, who had flown in from Tuscaloosa. It was an early morning reporting time of 5:00 a.m. in order to be prepped and to get in cue for what promised to be a long day. Randy voiced a prayer with us, and we were on our way.

Once at MDA, it was all business as they readied me for surgery, and soon, right on schedule, they said it was time to travel to the OR (operating room). It was a calm peace that settled in over us as everyone bid me their best wishes for a successful operation. Oh, there had been moments of apprehension, fears, and worry about the unknown outcome that this day would bring. Undoubtedly each of us secretly wondered what the new Mark would be like that emerged from this complex operation. But today was only one event of many that our God had scripted into my journey in which He would make Himself known.

Back on the gurney, it was the true image of total surrender—when they wheel you out and away from all of your loved ones and into a cold, bright, sterile operating room full of total strangers who will be slicing and wreaking medically acceptable havoc to your face, neck, head, and perhaps brain over the day ahead. You realize that you are totally out of control of the situation and are dependent on a team of medical professionals along with a myriad of devices and equipment designed to facilitate a successful operation and desired outcome. But there was nothing that I could do but silently voice one more prayer for God to reign over my surgery and its outcome. Suddenly, I faded into a restful sleep. The sedative had taken effect. The daylong procedure had begun.

Lindsay would later marvel at the crowd that assembled that day in the waiting room: immediate family, college friends, cousins, dear friends from the past—most of whom traveled a long way just to be there to lend support. She realized how blessed we were and commented how rare it is these days to witness that level of support. As the day dragged on, it was that group, along with the prayers of others from around the world, that would help sustain she and Lesa and help to pass the time.

The surgical team would also provide frequent updates on their progress. The first good news was that the neurosurgeon would not be needed, and he was dismissed from the procedure. Throughout the day, other families would occupy the waiting area, but as day turned to night, my group was the only one remaining. As they turned out the lights in the waiting area, the news came that I was out of surgery, bypassing recovery, and would soon be in my room.

After confirming that I had come through the procedure OK, my support group began heading out to their respective homes or hotels to get some deserved rest. My brother, Steve, offered to stay the night with me, giving Lesa and Lindsay a much-needed break. The journey through recovery had now begun.

CARINGBRIDGE® JOURNAL ENTRY #17
JULY 3, 2015

SURGERY DAY RECAP

Hi! It's Lindsay. I'm following through with the tasks assigned to me by Dad yesterday. They were (in no particular order) the following: take care of Mom, deposit some checks, and write CaringBridge® update. But I warn you, if you think my writing will be half as entertaining as my Dad's, well then as we say in the South, "bless your heart." That gene may not have passed down.

Here goes nothing, though . . .

All in all, the day went better than the doctors expected! They were able to completely remove the mass, and it showed minimal involvement of surrounding tissue and bone. It has been sent for pathology, and we hope to know some answers in a week or so. There will likely be follow-up treatment of some sort. Radiation has been thrown out, but we really won't know specifics until later. We're just rejoicing tonight that the sucker is out of there!

Each of our three surgeons was pleased with the way things progressed. I say three because the neurosurgeon was not needed after all! They came out individually and spoke with us, and again, we were all reminded what gifted specialists we are working with here.

Recovery begins now, and it won't be a walk in the park. (See what I did there? You thought I wasn't gonna be able to think of a clever "walking" analogy. *BOOM!*) He did not have to go to the ICU but is resting now in a regular room, which we know is the best way for his body to heal. We ask for you to continue praying specifically for the wound sites to heal, tissues to connect properly, and for Dad's willpower and stamina. Pray for our family and dear friends who have been with us today. We could all use some rest.

My head is tired, friends, and I'm quite sure I have left out some very important details, but I hope you'll forgive me. It was a very intense day to say the least. But we absolutely felt carried by your prayers. For that, we cannot say thank you enough.

Thanks for walking, or sitting, or praying, or celebrating with us today!

CARINGBRIDGE® JOURNAL ENTRY #18
JULY 4, 2015

INDEPENDENCE DAY

I t's Lindsay again.

To celebrate the July 4th holiday, Dad is buying cupcakes for the nurses. Surprised? Me neither.

Our other celebration was a very determined and successful lap around the nurses' station! On a day where I know he would probably much rather stay in bed, he has walked not once but twice. They were also able to remove a couple of tubes, which was a welcomed change. He still has the tracheostomy and feeding tube which make communicating difficult, but we are slowly developing our own "Wiggins family hand signals" to try and keep him well taken care of. I can't imagine how frustrated he has been at times, but he is hanging in there like a champ.

All total, he will probably be in the hospital for about a week, but he is making great strides (quite literally), and we are all extremely proud! Please continue to pray that his body heals as it should.

Thank you for walking with us today!

***

Back home in Memphis, another story was unfolding . . .

July 4th began as a routine holiday weekend. Whitney and family went to watch the city-sponsored fireworks show that night. She went to bed feeling "kind of crampy." By 1:00 a.m. her stomach started hurting really bad, and she got up and lay on the couch, willing the pain to go away. As the sun rose, things only worsened, and she was getting lightheaded from the pain. She called a neighbor, kissed her girls goodbye, and headed off to the ER.

On the way, she texted Lindsay with her circumstances and told her not to tell Mom. Lindsay was at the hotel after having spent the previous night with me at the hospital and getting little rest. After getting out of the shower and getting ready to come back to the hospital, she noticed an inbound text on her phone lying on the bed. She later tearfully remembered reading the text and punching out the pillows on the bed in frustration. *How can this be? Why? Why now?*

Whitney would end up spending an awful day in the ER and a painfully uncomfortable night in the hospital after the surgeon determined they would have to perform a do-over of a previous abdominal surgery due to intestines twisting and adhering to the mesh that only a year earlier had mended her own benign tumor excision.

Being a mother herself and knowing that she would want the knowledge that her child was facing a critical surgery, Lindsay made another right decision to fully disclose to Lesa what was going on back in Memphis. With me recovering well at MDA, it had already been determined that Lindsay would return to parenting duties back home in Dallas later that morning. With wisdom and maturity, she broke the shocking news to her mother, and Lesa assured her that she would tell me at the "appropriate" time, considering that I was still vastly under the effect of post-surgery meds.

Back home, friends, family, our church, and neighbors all went into action to take care of kids and maintain a sense of normalcy. Oh, what blessings in such a time of need!

In retrospect, this was just another manifestation of God's hand in the details of our family's journey. It pained Whitney so greatly that she was not by her daddy's side for his surgery. But

God placed obstacles in the way that prevented her from traveling to Houston. And, had she gone on and made the trip, she would have been facing emergency surgery of her own—far away from the doctors that knew her fragile condition and the details surrounding her previous surgery.

CARINGBRIDGE® JOURNAL ENTRY #19
JULY 11, 2015

WALKING . . . BLESSED

From Lesa: This post references yesterday, 7/9/2015:

Dearest friends, family, and faithful prayer warriors,

To God be the glory. To the amazement of the medical team here at MDA, Mark has been discharged. *The Great Physician* has brought us to this junction of the road, and we are blessed. Our lead doctor came into the room this morning and asked Mark if he wanted to go home. *Well, duh* . . . Things progressed very quickly. Trachea tube removed, feeding tube removed, IV removed. He is a free man.

We were able to go to our temporary home at the Rotary House adjacent to the hospital. I had made reservations here earlier last week but had no idea when we would go home. I had made them in *hopes* of being released. This hotel stay was booked at least three weeks in advance. The Lord has provided us this place through Monday. I have asked for prayers to extend our stay here a few days because of doctor's appointments next week and the convenience of clinic access. We always have the option of going back to the RV, but Mark will have difficulty making the high step into the doorway.

Mark is mobile with the help of a walker. The incision on his upper leg where the muscle was taken is approximately twelve to fourteen inches long. This causes him to be unstable. We had no idea it would be so large, but it is only a minor inconvenience . . . considering. The surgical area in the jaw and neck is healing well. The twelve-hour surgery was complicated, but we are blessed things went well. We were not surprised by anything about the surgery and its results, except—*no need for a neurosurgeon. Praise the Lord.*

Do you believe in miracles? *I do.* You have just been traveling on a journey filled with them. *The Great Physician* has shown us His mighty power to heal. Giving thanks!

I have said many times that Whitney and Mark are *tight,* but, seriously, the hospital and surgery at the same time is a bit much! Whitney continues to improve daily. It was a "race" to see who could cross the finish line first, and Mark won, but Whit continues to *run* the halls of Baptist Hospital in Memphis. Thanks to so many of you for being her mama when I could not be there. A special thanks goes out to my sister, Kathy, who has stepped in to be mama and grandmother to my granddaughters. And if you know those girls, she has her hands *full.*

Am I rambling again? Indulge me. I am so excited and wish I could hug each one of you personally. If you come to Houston, *I will!* Until then, to quote Elvis, "Thank you . . . thank you very much!"

I believe and continue to pray for miraculous healing *for God's glory.* Praying to amaze the doctors here with a benign pathology report and to return home—*cancer free.* Believing.

My thanks also to each of you traveling with us for all your prayers, words of encouragement, and just being there for us. I love you all.

Thanks for walking with me today!

—Lesa

CARINGBRIDGE® JOURNAL ENTRY #20
JULY 11, 2015

WALKING IN PRAISE

T his is from Lesa . . .

Dearest friends, family, and faithful prayer warriors,

Today my heart is filled with praise. *Thank You, Jesus.* Yesterday was another day of miracles on our journey. When we woke up yesterday morning, *Superman* decided to ditch the walker and walk unassisted. Then, why should we stay in the hotel where so many people need rooms? Amid all the hurting people here at MDA, we are incredibly blessed. Pray continuously that cancer be killed at the root. Many people are suffering.

We returned to the RV and *Superman* made the steps in a single bound (well, maybe I stretched that a little, but he made it!). We settled in, and then we were off to do a little shopping—grocery shopping!

When we got back, I realized I did not have my wallet. So what did I do? I fell on the floor and bawled. We called Kroger. Miracle number one: I saved the receipt. The manager said no one had turned one in. He even looked on the surveillance cameras and saw me pay for the groceries and walk out, and I still had my wallet in my hand. He even knew what color my dress was. *Scary.*

We left Mark's cell number, and then I was on my knees on the floor *praying.* I guess I had the wrong order! Within a matter of minutes, the manager called and said someone had turned in my wallet—miracle number two: they had found it in a cart outside. We were off.

When we arrived, the manager (the one who had checked me out and whom we had talked to on the phone) still had my wallet in his pocket and told us a dear old lady had found it and given it to him. He thought she was still in the store, and so we searched the aisles to give her our thanks. She was nowhere to be found. Do you believe in angels? *Thank You, Jesus!*

After we returned home, I just wanted to shut the door and stay inside. My day was *done.* I had all I could handle. At least, so I thought. *Superman* decided we needed to go for another walk. The man is wearing me out, but, as he said, for the first time in my life, my short legs can walk faster than him! I'm sure that won't last long.

Mark ate a microwave meal of potatoes and mystery meat, but it is soft, and he can eat it. Another miracle. That may be the best eighty-seven cents we have ever spent. Busy day. Filled with miracles. *Thank You, Jesus.*

Next week is filled with follow-up appointments, speech therapy, etc. On Wednesday we have our appointment with Dr. Myers, the lead surgeon of the team. It will have been at least ten days post-op, and pathology reports should be in. I guess you all know me well enough to know what is on my mind. *I trust You, Jesus.*

Dr. Myers has said all along he thought it was cancer, so I am trying to prepare myself. I also know *the Great Physician* has been in control of every step of this journey, and, as the song goes, "Our Lord will show up; and He will take you through the fire again!"[3] Praying for a miraculous healing *for God's glory.* Believing.

Whitney continues to improve. They are at my house because her kitchen is scheduled to be painted this week. Yes, that was scheduled well in advance of the latest adventure. My sister, Kathy

---

3. Lyrics by the Crabb family, "Through the Fire," 2000.

(another angel), will be going home this weekend. She has stayed at the hospital every day while Ben, Whitney's husband, goes to work. He kept Mary Collins and Nora every night and took them to school before heading to the hospital. *Thank You, Jesus!* Whitney will be off work for at least two weeks. She is *Superwoman* but cannot pick up the girls or other household duties, obviously. Thanks for all who have signed up to take her a meal. *Blessed.*

It's a new day, and I am sure *Superman* will have on his cape and be ready to fly. He continues to gain strength and is making improvements day by day. *Thank You, Jesus,* and thank each one of you for your prayers, emails, texts, and kind words of encouragement. No way we could travel this road without you. We are *blessed.*

Great is the Lord and most worthy of praise; his greatness no one can fathom. (Psalm 145:3)

Thanks for walking with us.

—**Lesa**

CARINGBRIDGE® JOURNAL ENTRY #21
JULY 15, 2015

WALKING AGAIN . . . ALBEIT SLOWLY

I'm back! I look forward to resuming our journey together.

After surgery on July 2, I spent six days in the hospital at MDA and was released last Wednesday afternoon to recover here in the Houston area. It was an amazing experience to hear and witness God at work through the details of my surgery, post-op, and subsequent recovery, as well as the other subplots of this story, which I will save for later commentary. Although I am slowly getting back to normal (whatever that is), I am still having lingering effects of the anesthesia which, for what was needed for a twelve-hour surgery, were pretty massive doses. So I have relied on my support team to communicate in my "absence," and they have done a great job.

So before I move on with updates, let me share with you a couple of lessons that this experience has taught me thus far, and I am sure many more will follow . . .

1. Outside of the gift of salvation through Jesus Christ and a relationship with Him, I am convinced that good health is God's next greatest gift and one that we must never take for granted. I know that I have in the past and heretofore

been blessed with good health. So join me in starting a practice of giving thanks each day for the sheer ability and opportunity of sucking in lungs full of air and for bodies that amazingly process and thrive in spite of our treatment and abuse of them.

2. Living a healthy lifestyle does not make you immune to sickness and disease. Although I have been repeatedly told that my distance running and overall physical condition would certainly play to my favor throughout this ordeal, I shudder to think what it would have been without the previous conditioning.

3. The effect of the countless prayers, emails, texts, posts, calls, and other acts of compassion can only be comprehended by one who has been through similar fires himself and has understood firsthand what it means to be on the receiving end of such an incredible outpouring. We are humbled by your showing of love and concern, and it has affected me profoundly. While saying "thank you" alone seems so trite, I want you to know that every one of those gestures will be forever recorded on our hearts and that just the simplest showing of love has been deeply appreciated. The next time you stop and think, *Well, I should do this or that for someone*, go ahead and take action and do it, because the redemptive value of that gift is immeasurable.

I am amazed at the human body and how it can bounce back from the major trauma like mine did two weeks ago. I am also amazed at how it will make you pay for putting it through said trauma. Let me just say that anyone who desires to take me on for a race should step up right now, because you would be assured a win.

And so the journey continues. I remember back a few months ago when checking in for blood work at MDA for the first time. I scanned the crowd and was astounded by people of all tribes and nations—a melting pot of diversity. While there were easily over a hundred people crammed into the waiting rooms, spilling out into the hallways, and the elevator lobby space is standing room only, the sign on the wall claimed a wait time of no more than thirty minutes. *Yeah, right,* I thought . . . as my mind recalled recent customer service conversations with "Bob" in India. But in typical MDA form, their efficiency was at work, and it became clear that they would deliver on the promise of thirty minutes or less or you get your blood back (no, not really). All of us there with a common need, anxiously waiting our name—all ages, all demographics, all body types, and all conditions, apparently whole, and some clearly bearing the signs of aggressive surgery directly resulting from their cancer. I was reminded in that moment that this could be a long journey.

Well, today we learned of the next phase of that journey. My official diagnosis, which we have been in search of since arriving here in late April, has been determined to be sarcomatoid carcinoma of salivary gland origin. Don't waste your time in Googling it, as it is a rare form (family, can I recall the "strive to be exceptional in everything you do" speech? It is due for a severe re-edit!). The treatment will be a regimen of proton radiation therapy combined with induction chemotherapy. The two will run simultaneously, with chemo one day a week and radiation five days a week. We are tentatively scheduled to begin in early August and will run approximately six weeks.

While God has not performed our miracle of choice, *He is at work* through the hands of the skilled team at MDA, and our confidence continues to be emboldened by His many acts of faithfulness to date. Keep believing . . . I know we are!

> *Then Jesus said, "Did I not tell you that if you believe, you will see the glory of God?" (John 11:40)*

Thanks for walking with me today!

CARINGBRIDGE® JOURNAL ENTRY #22
JULY 30, 2015

WALKING AGAIN...PICKING UP THE PACE

This October marks the tenth anniversary of the first and only full marathon I've run, although I have completed a dozen or so halves. It was one of the early Walt Disney World (WDW) marathons, and they pulled out all the stops to advertise the magic of what running in this event would entail. Picture yourself running down Main Street, through Cinderella's Castle, in addition to running through all five theme parks. Of course, it all happens before the park opens, which means you have it all to yourself (well, you and twenty thousand other runners).

I clearly remember the feeling of accomplishment in having completed the first half of the marathon and the euphoria of seeing that split in the course that led to the finish line for the half marathon only a few hundred yards away—next to the signs pointing to our path for completing the full. Another 13.1 miles ahead. In many ways, it is like the journey I now find myself in: so much accomplished, looking over my shoulder, and yet so much still ahead. A successful surgery to remove a fist-sized tumor is behind me; yet in order to complete the race and finish strong, this second half will require all the faith, courage, and strength that I can muster. Radiation and chemotherapy lie ahead.

Those of you who have trained for distance running know that you typically don't run the full distance in your training runs leading up to the event, and certainly that was true for my full marathon. So much of the second half of that race that lie ahead was virgin territory—untested, untried, unproven, and unknown.

Like mile fifteen of the Disney Marathon. Disney is an incredible corporation and very environmentally conscious. So one would not find it odd that they have their own sewage treatment facility—and, you guessed it, mile fifteen takes you right by it. (No, this was not mentioned in the brochure!) Just as you are settling in to the fact that you have as far to go as you have come thus far, an endless cloud of methane gas smacks you right in the face, grabs your lungs, and will not let go. It was as if all one hundred fifty thousand guests that would visit the parks that day had flushed at the same time. I've never had an up close and personal encounter with a skunk, but that had to be what it is like.

But there's more! Just as you begin to reach clean air again and your nostrils start to trust you once more, you reach mile seventeen: the composting facility (I told you they were serious tree huggers!). After all, why let those tons of waste go to waste? Actually, this part of the race probably reflects some of the better average paces because everyone is doing their best to run away from the stench!

So that's where I find myself today: approaching miles fifteen to seventeen in my journey at MDA. Radiation and chemo are ahead, and, from what I've been told, they're both gonna stink really bad. But, just as in the WDW Marathon, they are part of the journey (expected or not) and must be completed in order to finish the race.

Whitney and I did finish the race that day and promptly vowed to each other to stick with half marathons from then on. But it was what happened between miles twenty-two and twenty-three that provides a good "ending" to today's post.

Distance running takes its toll on one's body. Part of the reason you train so long is not only to develop endurance but also to be able to understand and predict your body's response to the abuse. Long before mile twenty-two we'd already resorted to alternately running and walking to help manage the limited stores of energy we both had left. The theme parks were far behind us, and we were pounding it out on the endless myriad of service roads that encircle the properties. Of course in Disney, "larger than life" fashion, the service roads are like interstate roadways. And it was somewhere between twenty-two and twenty-three that it hit me—you know, that moment when nature calls and you are faced with an immediate decision, with no good options. The nearest porta potty was perhaps a mile or two away, and the flashbacks of the sewage treatment plant I'm having (though now eight miles behind us) is only exacerbating the problem. *This is not going to be pretty*, I said to myself.

I told Whitney that I would catch up to her and headed off course and up a bluff that had a sparse population of pines. Of course, at Disney, even the right of ways are groomed and landscaped. Having reached the ascent but finding no cover, I desperately dropped my running shorts, assumed a squat, and found relief with no time to spare.

It was somewhere between almost passing out and finishing my prayer of deliverance that the noise alerted my senses back to my situation. It was a rumble, then a hiss. No, multiple rumbles and hisses. Surely that can't be what it sounds like. I meekly looked over my shoulder to discover what was on the other side of the precipice. There, in clear view to me and me to them, was the employee parking lot with their transport buses at morning rush hour. In my rush to find relief, and in an effort to modestly shield myself from any runners on the course who may have witnessed my dilemma, I'd instead mooned most of the Walt Disney cast! I don't know if there's a Guinness Book of Records entry for the largest mooning at WDW, but I may have earned it that day with no effort intended.

Thanks for walking with me today!

CARINGBRIDGE® JOURNAL ENTRY #23
AUGUST 11, 2015

WALKING INTO THE UNKNOWN

It's time to man up (or wo-man up, if you are of the female gender and still with me on this journey). Today's the day. The first of thirty radiation blasts kicks off today at 12:00 p.m. Houston time followed by the first of six cycles of chemotherapy beginning Thursday at 4:45 p.m. Radiation will repeat weekdays while the chemo is administered weekly . . . then you are left to deal with the aftermath until the following week. Your prayers are greatly appreciated, and we ask specifically that the treatments be effective, with little or no side effects, and again that there would be no collateral damage that would impair the great recovery that is already underway since surgery—now six weeks behind us.

I can safely say that in many ways, I am back to normal. I know that comes as a disappointment to some of you . . . particularly after hearing there were both plastic surgeons and neurosurgeons involved, and you were hoping for more. Perhaps it only made sense that improvements should be in order. But just as you can't judge a book by its cover, I can tell you that one does not survive a journey such as this one without walking away forever changed. So hopefully you'll notice improvements after all.

In business, as parents, or as students, you are expected to know the answers. The staff here at MDA has provided great information and resources regarding what to expect from both the radiation and chemo treatments, although still unknown is how both will affect me. I have to admit that I still have more questions than answers when it comes to this mysterious cancer that has chosen to attack me. But, you know, in some ways, it's great not having to have all of the answers. That's a part of the journey of faith—when you stop relying on the known and trust your unknowns with the One who best knows you and what is best for you. It's like it was when you were a child, and you didn't have to sweat the details because your mom or dad did that for you. Life was merely yours to enjoy. Can that be one of the hidden blessings that comes from this mess we have been dealing with . . . a return to that level of faith and reliance that results in the peace and joy of seizing the moment?

The last couple of weeks have been filled with appointments in a variety of disciplines, from physical and occupational therapists to speech therapists, nutritionists, and others, to help me fully recover and adapt to the changes taking place post-surgery and with the two upcoming treatment regimens. Now that the action has resumed here at MDA, I will try to be more faithful to share with you. Until then, keep walking!

Thank you for walking with me today!

CARINGBRIDGE® JOURNAL ENTRY #24
SEPTEMBER 1, 2015

WALKING IN PRAYER

My apologies for the lack of communication since my last post. I really do feel an obligation to keep you informed of my status since you have been so faithful to keep us in your prayers. Radiation and chemo have both been manageable so far, but part of my reluctance in reporting that is that things could change quickly. For example, it's early in week four of treatment and sores have formed in my mouth and throat as a side effect of the radiation, making it particularly hard to swallow. This was to be expected, but that doesn't make it more tolerable. This affects not only food intake but hydration as well. It has been a full-time job keeping up with caloric intake, fluid intake, and protein intake, and ensuring that I am voiding all of the above on a consistent and regular basis. Not to mention the exercises from speech pathology, head and neck post-op and radiation exercises, and the physical therapy at-home regimen that is to be done—all with waning stores of energy. Completing those can be a challenge at times, but I have been able to maintain my two-mile walk in the morning and another two in the evening. It's my own personal measure of how I am doing.

Beyond the physical aspects, I'm finding that "chemo brain" is real—disabling me from doing many things that otherwise would be simple. And yes, one of those is writing, so I beg for your indulgence until the fog clears. Between it and the other side effects, I constantly want to move the clock up three weeks in an effort to get this behind us. But I must force myself to keep the focus on the present and take it one day at a time.

Your prayers are appreciated and have been both felt and answered in so many ways. I couldn't ask for better training partners. Keep up the great work!

Answer me when I call to you, my righteous God. Give me relief from my distress; have mercy on me and hear my prayer. (Psalm 4:1)

Thank you for walking with me today!

CARINGBRIDGE® JOURNAL ENTRY #25
SEPTEMBER 11, 2015

WALKING IN TRUTH

The LARGEST MEDICAL COMPLEX IN THE WORLD . . . the NUMBER ONE CANCER CENTER IN THE WORLD . . . the LARGEST CHILDREN'S HOSPITAL IN THE WORLD . . . the LARGEST CONCENTRATION OF MEDICAL PROFESSIONALS IN THE WORLD. The ad reads like a virtual who's who, or should I say where's where, further reminding us that we are exactly where we need to be to stage this part of our fight.

One of the many things that I have learned in my five-month involvement with MDA is that if they put it in print, you can pretty well bank on it as truth. The same holds true when it comes to my treatment—it has been "as advertised." One could say that with the vast cautionary claims that are made up front, that they have covered the waterfront when it comes to anything that could happen. But my medical specialists have narrowed those to the ones that I can realistically expect to encounter, and they have been spot on. I am realizing that the severity of each will vary according to my particular body chemistry and make up, which is another reminder that God has fearfully and wonderfully made us. (Read all of Psalm 139, which includes this assurance and so much more.)

So yes, the side effects that I am dealing with have worsened as I enter week five of chemo (yesterday)—mouth and throat sores, pain, lack of appetite, nausea (but no vomiting, so I feel I am winning there!), and further weight loss. Energy levels are declining due to the above. As the speech therapist said yesterday, the first couple of weeks are unfair to you because they lull you into a sense of having little issues when all it is doing is piling those onto the back end of treatment. And you get to carry this misery home with you for the two to three weeks following the point when treatment ends. As I stated in a post a couple of weeks ago, we have definitely entered the endurance phase of our marathon.

So even with all of the above ratings and acclaim, when the pathology reports finally came back in late July, the esteemed team at MDA was still stumped. "The *truth*," they said, "is that you have an extremely rare form of salivary gland cancer" (one claim is that there are only another forty-two or so recorded cases). "The *truth* is that there is little data on it, making selecting effective treatment protocols a challenge. So we need to deal with it based on what is known (*truth*). The treatment used will be what we know to be effective based on other salivary gland origin cancers and based on much more extensive data (*truth*). And that is what we have done."

Do you know *truth* when you see it? In John 14:6, "Jesus answered, 'I am the way and the *truth* and the life. No one comes to the Father except through me" (emphasis added).

Thank you for walking with me today!

CARINGBRIDGE® JOURNAL ENTRY #26
SEPTEMBER 24, 2015

WALKING WITH HELP

Have I mentioned that my wife is amazing? She has not only assumed much of my "job" of shared parenting, but she has been my full-time caregiver, which in this particular setting and under these conditions, is not something that I would wish on anyone. But God has blessed me with an incredible woman to be alongside me for this particular journey (actually, I have been the beneficiary of this blessing for our journey together of thirty-eight years and pray for many, many more years to come). She has been my advocate, spokeswoman, personal driver, and loving and patient spouse particularly over the last few weeks as my side effects have grown to be more of a test. I can attest that it has not been fun for her—as much as she longs that my every need be met. Between treatments, appointments, procedures, and therapies, it has wreaked havoc on her normally active and structured lifestyle. *Lesa, there is no way that I can thank you enough, even if my voice and mouth would cooperate. In addition to everything else you do with your usual level of excellence, you can now add nursing to the list.*

Last Thursday, I rang the bell signifying my last chemotherapy infusion. On Tuesday night, I struck the gong concluding my thirty sessions of proton therapy. Yesterday I had a procedure to insert a feeding tube, which will help me begin the process of gaining some of the weight back and supplying the hydration and nutrition that are both sorely needed. While each of these accomplishments were reasons to celebrate, those days were among the hardest I have faced. But even though the week after treatment ends is as brutal as they cautioned, I am beginning to sense that we are days away from busting out of here. Your continued prayers are coveted as we hope to see further improvement—one day at a time!

Thank you for walking with me today!

CARINGBRIDGE® JOURNAL ENTRY #27
SEPTEMBER 30, 2015

WALKING WITH UNDERSTANDING

There's a quote placed on the desk of my home office that is scripted in my own lousy handwriting. Although it has been there for years, I'm not sure where it came from or the circumstances that caused me to scribble it onto a 3 x 5 index card. It is a quotation from Dr. Sam Peeples. I don't know Dr. Peeples. I'd never heard of him before or since then, although I am sure a quick Google search could enlighten me as to his background and credentials. But it was not knowledge of him that got my attention but rather his words. The saying reads as follows: *The circumstances of life, the events of life, and the people around me in life do not make me the way I am, but* reveal *the way I am.*

That pretty well says it all. It's not the stuff that life throws at us but rather the stuff we are made of to deal with it that will ultimately surface and drive our response.

For me, that has helped answer all of the *Why* questions. Situations such as these afford those of us who are believers the opportunity to try and live out by example the faith and hope we have in Jesus Christ. For me, if, by going through all this cancer, by my example or my words only one person would be pointed to Jesus Christ and come to know Him, then it would have been worth it all—not only to know Him as Healer but also as the true source of life, the true source of hope, the true source of joy, and the true source of meaning.

My pace is picking up. Better days are ahead.

Thank you for walking with me today!

CARINGBRIDGE® JOURNAL ENTRY #28
OCTOBER 1, 2015

WALKING IN MEMPHIS

W*ho's a survivor?*
     You became a survivor on the day you were diagnosed.

The sign caught my eye my very first day at MDA. It's positioned on a wall to the left of the Head and Neck Cancer Treatment Center check-in area and level-sets your expectations from the start. I'm sure it is not the only one of its kind because the message is what resounds from this institution.

Well it looks as though the finish line for me has been pushed out into the future. While this race together is now complete, I have been blessed with more days to walk, to run, and hopefully to have an impact. We leave MDA and Houston today, having experienced the healing hand of God at work through the hundreds of doctors, nurses, technicians, and staff that crossed our path and who helped in restoring me to health. I thank God for them and for those of you who tirelessly and faithfully struggled along with me on this journey of faith.

I came here a blessed man already. I had the resources, had the connections to help fast track treatment, and was able to step away from work to focus on getting well. And I had the unbounded support of family and friends. To be honest with you, at times I would have taken some or all of these for granted. One of my new blessings is renewed appreciation for the value of those gifts.

Although I hope this to be my last journal update until follow-up examinations at year end, my CaringBridge® account will remain open, so you are welcome to post.

My gratitude knows no end! Thanks again for walking with me on this journey. Godspeed to you on yours.

***

Two weeks after returning to Memphis, I attended my sixtieth birthday party, which was given by my wife and kids to celebrate this milestone but also to reintroduce me into post-cancer life back in Memphis. It was a gala affair at a local country club with over one hundred fifty friends and family attending. I felt so much gratitude, both for the love and friendship shown that night but also for my wife and children—each of whom knew the status of my condition and that I was really not physically up to it and still pressed on with the event. Besides the physicality, I'm just not one to have attention drawn to me, so I was reluctant from the earliest discussion about the party.

The two weeks after ending radiation and chemo were exactly as they said it would be. You would feel cruddy. Radiation would still show signs of the "burn" that had taken place far below the surface. Combine this with chemo and you were assured of seemingly never-ending mucositis flow in your mouth and throat.

All of this would wreck your appetite when you needed it most to try to rebuild and replenish what had been taken away by this harsh treatment. So with all of this baggage, I dressed up in my finest party attire and put on my happy face—as wretched as it was—and prepared for the night ahead.

Now you have to remember that I had dropped between fifty and sixty pounds since the beginning of this malady, so nothing in my wardrobe was "suitable." So the week before the party, I reluctantly made the trip to a favorite haberdashery to be fitted for a new suit that hopefully would not fit after another couple of months. The only alteration needed was for the pants to be hemmed. So pickup was scheduled for Wednesday of the following week—two days before the event.

Wednesday rolled around, and, presenting my alterations claim ticket, I picked up the suit, and then once home, promptly hung it in my closet for use on Friday night.

As the party time drew near that night, Lesa and the sons-in-law headed to the country club to make sure everything was ready and as planned. One of these details was placement of the portable vacuum pump that was my constant companion to help vacuum away the mucous that continuously accumulated in my mouth and throat. It was placed under the family table at my designated seat in the corner of the ballroom, where I'd hoped to discreetly use it as often as necessary. The daughters and grandkids would accompany me a few minutes later. It would be about a twenty-minute trip.

Of course, I waited for the last minute before changing clothes. Unzipping the garment bag, I slipped the coat off of its hanger and laid it on the bed. I took the pants and placed one foot into the appropriate leg. It seemed like my foot continued forever before touching the ground. I methodically repeated the process with the alternate leg. Looking down as I pulled up the pants to my waist, it became clearly apparent that something was desperately wrong.

The pants were not hemmed!

No, not hemmed too long. No, not missing cuffs. The retailer's alteration department had done nothing in the week that had transpired since our purchase. But I would have to address their blunder at a later time—I was late for an important date!

In totally cool, "I've got this," fashion, Lindsay asked, "Do you have any duct tape?"

"Of course," I replied, "but why?"

Retrieving the roll, she made a quick measurement on the slacks and told me to slip them off. Turning under the exposed edge of each leg, she crafted a section of duct tape around the border of each leg on the inside and handed the slacks back to me. Perfect—well, almost.

With this near catastrophe addressed, I hurriedly began rounding up the grandkids to get loaded into the cars and off to the party. While doing so reminded me of herding cats, there seemed to be a particularly electric feeling in the air as the kids' noise and excitement level seemed to be amped up as they left the back door and headed onto the driveway. I locked the door and turned to join them, following in the direction of the screams. Looking up to find my designated seat, I stopped—something was not right. Instead of our minivan, at the end of the drive there was a stretch limousine! I was totally shocked.

It took very little coercion to get everyone onboard. There was no bickering over who was sitting where. The grandkids each picked "their" seat—either laying down in the seats, hanging out a window, or standing to pop up their heads through the open sunroof.

The fascination and enjoyment of their first limo ride continued until we arrived at the country club, pulling up under the portico to a red carpet entrance into the event. As the limo doors opened, live music from the stage band inside only added to the excitement. Stepping out reminiscent of a celebrity runway, no doubt the kids' minds were reeling: "Wow! Pa really knows how to throw a party!" The bar had been officially raised for future birthday celebrations.

Guests had already begun to arrive. Instead of being able to check out my seat and confirm the location of my "security blanket" suction pump, I was immediately surrounded by family, friends, coworkers, and church friends. Food lines were open, dance floor was open, band was playing . . . the party was officially on!

The next three hours flew by, and, until the last of the guests were making their way to leave, I was on my feet the entire time—either talking with guests, dancing with kids and grandkids, or generally working the crowd. It was a miracle in itself that I had the stamina to hold up. But the truly amazing miracle was for that whole time, I never once felt the need to visit the vacuum pump. Sipping on a glass of sweet tea kept those problems in check. And within a few days after that event, I retired the vacuum pump for good.

It was a miraculous night. Though things *seemed* to be destined to derail from the start, prayers for a truly special birthday event were abundantly answered.

CARINGBRIDGE® JOURNAL ENTRY #29
NOVEMBER 12, 2015

WALKING WITH CHRISTMAS CHEER

W e've been back in Houston this week for our first round of follow-ups. This will be a quarterly routine for the next year. Needless to say, our apprehension was palpable—not that we held doubts, but we were ready for our faith to be validated after the surgery, radiation, and chemotherapy.

So in the spirit of the season, here's our update:

3 Wise Men: A Modern Pilgrimage (that's a fancy word for journey)

Unlike in days of old when the wise men did the searching, our impatience prompted us to do our own "star" search. Leaving our hotel, we traveled east, having been told that was where the wise men were last spotted. And we found them, just as it had been foretold.

First was Morrison, the gray-haired sage. He offered the gift of good news of a clear CT scan—glad tidings of great joy, which will be made known to all people. This was a gift more valuable than pure gold!

Next, we sought out Myers, the wise and gifted surgeon. His gift was frank-and-made-sense. "Get out and exercise. Get back to living. And wean yourself from that feeding tube."

Finally came Masserrelli. This third magi is a wise *woman*—breaking the mold of the legendary three wise *men*. Her gift, the expensive chemo drug Cisplatin, had effectively done its part to eradicate all remaining cancer cells. So put the myrrh back on the shelf, people—it's so last century! Besides, we've got some livin' to do!

Happy Thanksgiving and a Merry Christmas to you. Both are coming early for us this year! Praise God for His goodness, His faithfulness, and how He has sustained us daily on this journey.

Thank you for walking with me today!

***

My kids both aged ten years in 2015. I could read it in their eyes—those big, beautiful brown eyes, from the genes they'd fortunately inherited from their mother. At times their shoulders bore the weight of insecurity as to what the future might hold without their daddy. Perhaps I'd "given them away in marriage" years before, but I still held both of them forever in my heart. And yes, I even noticed it in their sprigs of gray hair that began popping up prematurely. Although I had for years viewed them as adults (now both in their midthirties), perhaps they were for the first time coming to grips with their aging parents' mortality. While both of us are still young by today's standards, we'd been blessed with good health that had enabled us to maintain our youth and keep up with both the girls and four very active grandkids. That was our goal in having children while we were young. Sometimes in retrospect we'd questioned that we were ready to give parental instruction to children when in many ways we were both still kids.

But the lens was changed on how everyone was viewed in 2015. We were given a crash course in the many ways that a family can be attacked, and the things we held so dear seemed to be slipping out of our control. We relied deeply on each other in ways that we'd never known before. But many days it was our faith alone and the deep rooted belief that God would somehow turn tragedy into triumph that was the glue that kept it all together.

CARINGBRIDGE® JOURNAL ENTRY #30
FEBRUARY 17, 2016

WALKING AND WINNING

Today at MDA I walked with a more confident gait. Energy has started to return, albeit still a fraction of what I previously knew prior to the cancer, but I'll take the noticeable improvement. A part of that is the additional strides I've made to regain the fifty to sixty pounds of weight loss that the surgery, radiation, and chemo took from me. I weighed in today at 167 pounds, reaching a significant milestone—I now have less remaining to recover than I have already added back.

It is absolutely amazing the difference I've noticed since my last visit in November. While it pains me to see the suffering of those all around me, each of whom are in varying stages of their treatment or perhaps are bearing the pain of witnessing a loved one endure it, I now see my surroundings through a different lens—one of victory, success, and increased determination—and my joy is hard to contain. I'm among the fortunate survivors. We are beating this cancer! To see the hand of God at work throughout this journey is nothing short of miraculous!

Our scans yesterday once again showed no evidence of any recurrence. I'm good to go for another quarter.

Thanks again for walking with me today!

***

After the holidays, I had begun a weight training program at our church recreation facility. It was an effort to try and successfully manage the weight that was coming back in hopes that it would manifest itself as muscle and not fat. It was a three-day-per-week regimen that focused on both upper and lower body muscle groups, and I had started with lower weights and reps and gradually worked up as I could comfortably manage the more strenuous routine. It was hard to not get discouraged in those first few weeks as I worked with embarrassingly low weights that would easily tire me out. But those feelings faded as I started seeing results and feeling more like my old self.

Soon, I was ready for my next big test: resuming running. The intention was not to go out and try to set any new personal records but only to experience the thrill of just being back. Whitney joined me as she had started her own endurance effort. So we started out together on a familiar route that featured both uphill and downhill sections—away from my home but close enough to walk back if things got too demanding for either of us.

As we journeyed along at a consistent jog pace, we periodically took turns asking each other, "You OK?" The answer was always, "Yep," which bolstered both of our confidences. At one point midstride, Whitney commented that my biceps were getting bigger, affirming my workouts and further encouraging me to keep up the good work.

Having completed a successful outing and being the first to reach the house, I turned around to see her on the steps just behind me . . . crying . . . but tears of joy this time as she realized that the three miles we'd just run together were the first since I'd left for Houston and MDA some ten months before, since before the surgery, before the radiation and chemotherapy, before the months of separation, her own physical battles, and additional months of trauma that had left my body in the weakened state from the treatment's aftermath. For a precious moment, we embraced as the months quickly replayed in my mind in a rapid blur, and suddenly the journey seemed complete . . . it seemed that it had indeed been . . . a temporary inconvenience!

CARINGBRIDGE® JOURNAL ENTRY #31
MAY 2, 2016

CAUTION ... CURVE AHEAD

H OUSTON, TX:
The road took yet another turn this morning. What was anticipated to be a routine quarterly checkup at MDA ended up being everything but that.

CT scans revealed that my nemesis has returned. Cancer was found to have spread to my lungs. So it's more chemotherapy for me, but this time it will be administered by Dr. Al Weir back at home in Germantown, Tennessee.

There are many paths in life that will lead us to our final destination. Like a multilane expressway, paths do cross, and lanes do merge—sometimes due to construction, temporary detours, or being replaced by a new and better alternate route. On one of our early trips to Houston, I remember the frustration of sitting in six lanes of interstate highway traffic, which ultimately funneled down to a single exit ramp. It was so time consuming and appeared to be such a waste until it was finally our turn to ease from the barricaded roadway into the single lane exiting off the interstate and into unfamiliar surroundings. When we finally reached that bend in the road, the elevation of the exit ramp revealed a literal sea of floodwater from recent storms that had covered the interstate roadway ahead as far as we could see. It could not be seen from a driver's perspective until it would have been too late to avoid, which certainly would have resulted in an accident or perhaps even taken our lives.

What was initially interpreted as an inconvenience actually turned out to be another life-saving bend in the road. And while we don't understand why our journey has taken this latest turn, we trust and know that God's perspective is true and perfect, and what we can't see today, He has already finished. Our trust lies in Him to navigate us through the unfamiliar course that lies ahead. We stand confident that we're on the right path!

Jesus answered, "I am the way and the truth and the life. No one comes to the Father except through me." (John 14:6)

Thanks for walking with me again!

CARINGBRIDGE® JOURNAL ENTRY #32
MAY 16, 2016

WALKING A DIFFERENT PATH

Back to basics: just like when you have setbacks to your running or exercise plan, when the training resumes, you have to get back to the basics. With the significant improvements I'd seen over the past couple of months, I'd allowed myself to slip back into self-reliance and the false illusion that I am really back in control. We all know that is not the case.

Maybe the recurrence of my cancer is God's way of tugging at the reins to remind me that the bridle is still on, the bit is still in my mouth, and He not only knows the path that lies ahead but is fully in control of the obstacles we will face together. Sometimes I can be a stubborn mare, but what He really wants is for me to allow Him to make me the championship pedigree steed that He has created me to be.

On Wednesday I will begin a regimen of three kick-butt cancer drugs, one each day for three days, followed by an injection on Saturday to boost my immune system. Wednesday is a six-hour infusion, Thursday is four hours, and Friday only two hours. Then I will have a three-week break and repeat.

Join us in prayer that the side effects will be minimal, the drugs will be effective in arresting the cancer's growth, and even that God would choose to trump all of this with divine, miraculous healing in keeping with His will.

Thanks for walking with me today!

But blessed is the one who trusts in the Lord, whose confidence is in him. They will be like a tree planted by the water that sends out its roots by the stream. It does not fear when heat comes; its leaves are always green. It has no worries in a year of drought and never fails to bear fruit. (Jeremiah 17:7-8)

CARINGBRIDGE® JOURNAL ENTRY #33
MAY 20, 2016

WALKING LIKE A CHILD

L et me begin again with heartfelt thanks to everyone who has rallied behind us after learning our disappointing news of the recurrence two weeks ago. The outpouring of love has been simply humbling. While we were shocked with the diagnosis, we were not surprised by your loving responses. You've been faithful to walk this journey with us, regardless of where it has taken us or how long it has taken to get there.

Oh, for the faith of a child. This was sent to me shortly after learning that the cancer had spread to my lungs. It is from my friend Kim's five-year-old's prayer that night:

> *Mr. Mark has his cancer back, so I have to pray all night. God, please protect Mr. Mark and get his cancer out. Amen.*

Children really have it figured out when it comes to faith. They believe whole-heartedly, unconditionally, without trying to figure things out from a practical humanistic standpoint. In faith, they believe their dads can accomplish anything . . . and fix everything.

The modest home where I grew up sat on two acres of ground, the house itself occupying only a fraction of the front acre, leaving far too much grass for my brother and I to cut. The back acre was dedicated to my daddy's garden, from which most of our vegetables for the year were harvested. Along the back border of the garden was a barbed-wire-fenced path no more than four feet wide, just enough for our lone cow, Dolly, to move from the field where she spent her days grazing with a neighbor's herd to a very rudimentary shed, where she could be fed and milked while receiving some very basic protection from the elements at night. My job was keeper of the gate, and, late in the afternoon, I'd open the gate, let only Dolly in, and follow her to the pen and its shed.

As a child, that shed became my mental image of the Bethlehem stable, although comparing the two would be like comparing a Motel 6 to a five-star Four Seasons Hotel. This thing was ancient and rickety, and if a strong wind blew, it would probably all come tumbling down. There was room for two head of livestock max and a storage area across one end where feed and supplies were held.

One day, I determined to make improvements to Dolly's abode. There were numerous loose boards that appeared to be barely holding on, their nails clearly exposed as wood had aged and decayed over the years. I grabbed Daddy's hammer and a few nails and headed out for the child's version of *Home Improvement*.

I started with the most apparent need—the loose board on top that was attached only at one end. It should be an easy fix by just swinging the loose end back up and nailing it in place. While barely able to hold the weathered board in place, much less position the nail and then wield a man-sized hammer, I mustered a swing that landed squarely—on the board. The impact in fact was so great that it reverberated the entire length of the warped board, dislodging the other end that was previously nailed. Not to be discouraged, I laid the now totally free board to the side, thinking that I can come back to that one after "fixing" the rest.

In progression, I moved to the next board, which was totally intact, only bearing signs of age, rotted wood, and nails that once were firmly driven and had, over time, backed out, exposing much of the nail and revealing a prime target for a young boy looking to fix.

I attacked it with the hammer, this time managing no more than to severely bend the nail. *Surely a second blow would shore it up*, I thought. Wrong! The decayed wood around it crumbled, and I now had two boards lying at my feet.

Determined as I was for a fix, the process continued, but the results were the same. Looking back at the end of the afternoon, it looked more like demolition than restoration!

Defeated, I trudged tearfully back to the house to await Daddy getting home, being disciplined, and facing up to my fix-up gone bad.

Upon hearing my story, and in a totally unexpected response, Dad quietly picked up the hammer, found a few suitable nails, and headed back out with me to assess the damage. He took each damaged board, inspected areas that still had potential, and craftfully tapped the nails into wood that would hold. In a fraction of the time it had taken me to destroy the shed, he had put it all back together.

That childlike faith in our heavenly Father, so beautifully illustrated in Benjamin's prayer above, is what we all need to "fix" the ills in my life and in yours.

As I send you this update, I am completing my third day of chemo, and it has gone extremely well so far. I'll have a couple of weeks off, and then we will do it all over again. Keep the faith!

So in Christ Jesus you are all children of God through faith. (Galatians 3:26)

Thanks for walking with me today.

CARINGBRIDGE® JOURNAL ENTRY #34
JUNE 8, 2016

WALKING IN DAY-TIGHT COMPARTMENTS

His name is Lawrence McKinney. Like me, he's sixty years old. Unlike me, Lawrence spent thirty-one of his sixty years in prison. Convicted in 1978 of allegedly raping a woman and then stealing her television, he was sentenced to one hundred years in prison on the rape charge and another ten to fifteen for the burglary. In essence, he was given a death sentence, as he would certainly die in prison for his alleged crimes—crimes that he *did not* commit.

Yes, you read that correctly. McKinney was wrongly convicted and spent his twenties, thirties, forties, and early fifties incarcerated in a federal penitentiary before new DNA evidence cleared him, and he was then released in 2009.

In a recent *USA Today* interview, McKinney told the reporter this in response to his time in prison and his efforts to seek full exoneration from the governor (which still has not happened even seven years after his release): "I take things one day at a time, and I put my faith in the Lord. I know God has the last say-so."

I may have mentioned before that I only peruse the newspaper as opposed to my wife, Lesa, who reads every word (yes, I'm envious of her on a number of levels). But Mr. McKinney's article captivated me; both his response to the injustice that he endured and the outlook he has for his future speak volumes about his character and his faith. There's a lesson for all of us that comes out of his life experience—living one day at a time.

As a young sales guy in the early 80s, I had the opportunity to participate in a Dale Carnegie course. It was a fascinating and enlightening experience and one that I would highly recommend to anyone. While over time I have forgotten much of that curriculum, the following illustration has stuck with me, and I think of it often. In his book, *How to Stop Worrying and Start Living*, Carnegie tells the story of Dr. William Osler and how he lived a life consistent with Mr. McKinney's. Here's an excerpt from the book:

> *In the spring of 1871, a young man picked up a book and read twenty-one words that had a profound effect on his future. A medical student at the Montreal General Hospital, he was worried about passing the final examination, worried about what to do, where to go, how to build up a practice, how to make a living. The twenty-one words that this young medical student read in 1871 helped him to become the most famous physician of his generation. He organized the world-famous Johns Hopkins School of Medicine. He became Regius Professor of Medicine at Oxford—the highest honor that can be bestowed upon any medical man in the British Empire. He was knighted by the King of England. When he died, two huge volumes containing 1466 pages were required to tell the story of his life.*
>
> *His name was Sir William Osler. Here are the twenty-one words that he read in the spring of 1871—twenty-one words from Thomas Carlyle that helped him lead a life free from worry:*
>
> *"Our main business is not to see what lies dimly at a distance, but to do what lies clearly at hand."*
>
> *Forty-two years later, on a soft spring night when the tulips were blooming on the campus, this man, Sir William Osler, addressed the students of Yale University. He told those Yale students that a man like himself who had been a professor in four universities*

and had written a popular book was supposed to have "brains of a special quality." He declared that that was untrue. He said that his intimate friends knew that his brains were "of the most mediocre character."

What, then, was the secret of his success? He stated that it was owing to what he called living in "day-tight compartments." What did he mean by that? A few months before he spoke at Yale, Sir William Osler had crossed the Atlantic on a great ocean liner where the captain, standing on the bridge, could press a button and—presto!—there was a clanging of machinery and various parts of the ship were immediately shut off from one another— shut off into watertight compartments. "Now each one of you," Dr. Osler said to those Yale students, "is a much more marvelous organization than the great liner, and bound on a longer voyage. What I urge is that you so learn to control the machinery as to live with 'day-tight compartments' as the most certain way to ensure safety on the voyage. Get on the bridge, and see that at least the great bulkheads are in working order. Touch a button and hear, at every level of your life, the iron doors shutting out the Past—the dead yesterdays. Touch another and shut off, with a metal curtain, the Future—the unborn tomorrows. Then you are safe—safe for today! . . . Shut off the past! Let the dead past bury its dead. . . . Shut out the yesterdays which have lighted fools the way to dusty death. . . . The load of tomorrow, added to that of yesterday, carried today, makes the strongest falter. Shut off the future as tightly as the past. . . . The future is today. . . . There is no tomorrow. The day of man's salvation is now. Waste of energy, mental distress, nervous worries dog the steps of a man who is anxious about the future. . . . Shut close, then, the great fore and aft bulkheads, and prepare to cultivate the habit of a life of 'day-tight compartments.'"

Did Dr. Osler mean to say that we should not make any effort to prepare for tomorrow? No. Not at all. But he did go on in that address to say that the best possible way to prepare for tomorrow is to concentrate with all your intelligence, all your enthusiasm, on doing today's work superbly today. That is the only possible way you can prepare for the future.

Sir William Osler urged the students at Yale to begin the day with Christ's prayer, "Give us this day our daily bread." Remember that that prayer asks only for today's bread. It doesn't complain about the stale bread we had to eat yesterday; and it doesn't say: "Oh, God, it has been pretty dry out in the wheat belt lately and we may have another drought—and then how will I get bread to eat next fall—or suppose I lose my job—oh, God, how could I get bread then?" No, this prayer teaches us to ask for today's bread only. Today's bread is the only kind of bread you can possibly eat.[4]

In Psalm 118:24 (KJV) the scripture reads, *"This* is the day which the Lord hath made; we will rejoice and be glad in *it"* (emphasis added). Notice it does not say *tomorrow,* or *next week, next month,* or even *years from now.* It doesn't say *when I graduate, when I retire, when I have lost those twenty-five pounds, when I have ample money stashed away,* or even *when my health improves.* It says *"this* is the day." And that means now. I have the choice of how I will live today.

Today, for me, is day one of round two of chemotherapy here at the West Cancer Center. As I sit in my recliner along with as many as seven other patients at a time in this ward (it's one of several such arrangements in the chemotherapy infusion area), I'm looking up at the first four IV bags of the thirteen that I will get over the next six hours. I covet your prayers that the side effects are not experienced, that I maintain my weight and energy, that there is no compounding effect of this load of drugs along with the dose that I got three weeks ago, and yes, that God would grant healing. I'm convinced that my success in this treatment so far is due to the thousands of prayers that continue to be voiced on my behalf. I can never thank you enough, but I can encourage you to join me in living one day at a time in "day-tight compartments."

Thanks for walking with me today!

---

4. From HOW TO STOP WORRYING AND START LIVING, Revised Edition by Dale Carnegie. Copyright © 1944, 1945, 1946, 1947, 1948 by Dale Carnegie. Copyright renewed © 1984 by Donna Dale Carnegie and Dorothy Carnegie. Reprinted with the permission of Simon & Schuster, Inc. All rights reserved. Used with permission.

CARINGBRIDGE® JOURNAL ENTRY #35
JUNE 23, 2016

WALKING BLESSED, PART II

C ancer is a pain!
　　　Yet still, I am blessed—blessed with loved ones who dote over me from both near and far; blessed to not be besieged with problems of the workday, for many struggle with responsibilities of a job while fighting cancer as best they can; blessed that financial needs aren't an additional burden; and so thankful that I said yes to the agent that recommended disability insurance twenty years ago when, in perfect health, I thought to myself, *Rrriiigghhhttt!*

But cancer comes with blessings of a new perspective, or maybe just fresh ones that need to be revisited—like the reality that every day is indeed a gift and needs to be fully appreciated, now. That doesn't necessarily have to manifest itself in attempting to complete all of the things on our bucket lists but simply by soaking in the treasure of this day and realizing the goodness in it.

Blessings that you find in the strangest of places—like saving time when you no longer have to fix your hair or even have to mentally debate over how to wear it.

Blessings of relief from the oppressive Memphis summer heat thanks to my new cool hairstyle (or should I say "hairless" style).

Blessings that your face is always "kissable" because the stubble also went away with what was on top.

Blessings that the truth is finally out that my older brother and sister really did drag me around the house by my ears as a child, resulting in the satellite dishes that are affixed to either side of my head that can no longer be concealed by my hair. Busted, you two!

So, just to catch everyone up, I have had a manageable second cycle of chemotherapy for the lung cancer. Manageable in that I have breezed through the second batch of poisons with very few side effects. My oncologist continues to be amazed that I have fared as well as I have so far, considering the dosage and severity of the regimen. The lowest point for my white cell count just so happened to coincide with Father's Day weekend, so we opted to stay away from public places to avoid any possible infection, but I got to enjoy the kids and grandkids for the week anyway. This cycle was pretty much a do-over of the first one, and I am back to feeling strong and eating better with really no weight loss (OK, a couple of pounds, but that is negligible . . . unless you are trying to lose weight). Apparently I have grown so predictable that I do not have to go in for weekly blood work monitoring. Just show up for cycle three, which begins July 6 and will last three days.

Contrary to how I started this post, *no*, I am not in pain! Maybe it should be better put: *a temporary inconvenience.*

Oh, no, I did not forget. Another amazing blessing is that I have you on my team, praying for and supporting both me and my family in ways we can never forget. So thank you once again, and thanks for walking with me today!

But blessed is the one who trusts in the Lord, whose confidence is in him. (Jeremiah 17:7)

CARINGBRIDGE® JOURNAL ENTRY #36
JULY 24, 2016

WALKING WITH PATIENCE

Lord, give me patience . . . AND MAKE IT RIGHT NOW!
Can you relate? You'd think that after thirty-nine years of marriage, co-raising two kids, enduring four rambunctious grandkids, and surviving a career spanning over forty years, that I would finally have arrived at "Patience-topia." Though throughout this most recent phase of my journey, I have determined that it is not a destination we reach but rather a trait that is developed . . . and I believe that there is a reason that Paul, in his love letter to the Corinthians (1 Corinthians 13:1-13), lists patience first among the attributes of true love.

> *Love is patient, love is kind. It does not envy, it does not boast, it is not proud. It does not dishonor others, it is not self-seeking, it is not easily angered, it keeps no record of wrongs. Love does not delight in evil but rejoices with the truth. (1 Corinthians 13:4-6)*

He says it very clearly: "love is patient." Doesn't get more basic than that. And in my assessment, it's hard to really love without patience, and that patience has to come first. Because it's hard to reach those other attributes without first being patient . . .

- to be KIND to someone who is undeserving . . . when you aren't patient
- or to easily ENVY . . . when you aren't patient to fully understand the situation
- or even to BOAST or be PROUD of our accomplishments . . . without patience to realize that this, too, can change
- or to DISHONOR others . . . when we aren't patient enough to consider how we, ourselves, may respond in a similar situation
- or to SELFISHLY want to put ourselves first . . . when you don't have patience
- or to EASILY GET ANGRY . . . without patience to assess the appropriate level of emotion
- or to KEEP SCORE . . . when you don't have patience to remember that I'm not always right either

Perhaps the best illustration of patience can be seen in a cancer caregiver. It's hard to be patient when you long for healing and relief for your loved one that seems to never come; or when relief makes brief appearances only long enough to taunt you. It's difficult to be patient when, despite your incessant reminders of "what the doctor said," your pleas for confirmation of any signs of improvement seem to fall on seemingly unappreciative ears. And yet, in spite of these, the devoted caregiver patiently presses on. I know . . . I have one!

But if you continue reading that scripture, in verse seven it embodies the efforts of that caregiver:

> It [love] always protects, always trusts, always hopes, always perseveres. (1 Corinthians 13:7)

So among the things to include in your day-tight compartments, make sure to pack patience. As the saying goes, "*Time* is a great healer," and I am sure that patience has a lot to do with that.

The coming week continues to hold a true test of our patience as I look forward to a CT scan on Wednesday (7/27) that will determine our future course of action with regard to my treatment.

I have had three very aggressive (yet bearable) chemo sessions since moving treatment to The West Clinic here in Memphis, and it is time to assess their effectiveness. We covet your prayers always but particularly as we approach the scan and the results on Wednesday.

But for now, let's keep walking!

Be joyful in hope, patient in affliction, faithful in prayer. (Romans 12:12)

Thanks for walking with me today!

CARINGBRIDGE® JOURNAL ENTRY #37
JULY 28, 2016

WALKING WITH DISAPPOINTMENT

It was a crisp, cool October morning. Sunny . . . but cold enough to require layering to protect one from the frigid gusts that occasionally came out of the north. It was one of the earlier "Susan B. Komen Race for the Cure" 5Ks—a cause that was becoming a very popular and well-attended running event in Germantown, Tennessee, drawing thousands each year. Traffic had become a logistical challenge, and getting to the race site was best accomplished by parking in a remote location and shuttling in on one of the buses. Lesa and I climbed aboard our bus, only a couple of miles from the starting line. I was running the 5K race, and she was participating in the 1 Mile Family Fun Walk with friends. While we'd allowed ample time to make the short ride, it was quickly becoming apparent that this would be another record-setting crowd of runners and spectators that were assembling to show their support of breast cancer research and backing.

As we drew near the shuttle drop-off point, we concluded that the start time was rapidly approaching, and the herd was slowly migrating in that direction. When the bus unloaded, Lesa and I hurriedly parted for our respective starting points and agreed to meet "somewhere near the finish line." Somehow, neither of us was carrying our cell phones—an oversight that I would soon regret.

I made my way into the crowd. There was no warm-up jog, no stretching, and the temperatures with the wind chill reminded me that I had dressed far too scantily for this fall morning—three more things that would soon haunt me.

After a brief delay to help accommodate late arrivers, the starting horn for the 5K sounded, and the herd slowly started inching across the starting line. Now, understand, I am a seasoned runner but never expect to be standing on the podium to receive a prize based on my finish time. But I am very competitive in nature and always strive to set a personal record, or at least a respectable time for my age group (also keep in mind that this was several years ago). After all, 5Ks were a conditioning distance for me . . . sort of the minimum distance if I am going for a run.

As the thousands of runners began to pick up the pace and head down a long sloping hill, I observed that apparently some (no, many) of the participants failed to read the guidelines for the event, much less exhibited "race etiquette." There were walkers, mothers with strollers, dads with the twin pack strollers, and small children darting in, out, and among your feet like fire ants in a huge bed that has just been disrupted. Understand, these were all welcomed participants in this event, but all of the above are supposed to start at the back of the pack. Runners had to dart, weave, dodge, leap, stop/start, and otherwise maneuver over, around, and through this sea of flotsam before breaking free even for a jog pace. Of course, the small children were in an all-out sprint at this point, while continuing to bob and weave among my feet and legs. *Surely they will run out of gas soon*, I thought, but in effort to get clear of the pack, I, too, had inadvertently dialed up my speed prematurely, which was against my plan. My frustration was reaching the breaking point when I finally saw a clear lane that would allow me to distance myself from them and leave it all behind. Dialing it up a little more, I seized the opportunity. Now I am free to run *my* race.

Just as I was beginning to enjoy myself, and shortly after passing the MILE 1 marker, I felt the twinge in the back of my upper right leg. While continuing to run and mentally convince myself that it was nothing and would ease up as I warmed up, it hit. Feeling as if I'd been shot in the leg, I knew immediately that my right hamstring just blew. No warm up, no stretching, cold temperatures on exposed skin and muscles . . . my body was paying me back.

I moved to the side of the road and began to limp along toward my intended destination. I quickly concluded that I was done for the day, but I was not about to turn around and take the shortest distance back. Then they began to pass me—the dads with the twin pack running strollers, the small children, the mothers with strollers, even the walkers . . . only adding to the pain.

I resolved to make the best of a bad thing—to go on and finish the race that I'd started, albeit slowly and gingerly. With each grimacing step, I tried to convince myself to press on. By MILE 2, I was done, and I reluctantly decided to shortcut it back to the finish line. It would be the first (and only) race that I never finished.

Sweaty, cold, and under-dressed for the cold temperatures, I began the long and arduous search for my wife among the thousands of women wearing pink that day (remember . . . no cell phones!).

After an hour and a half, I located her and her friends near the finish line, looking for me and assuming that they'd missed me cross the line much earlier.

- It was a bad experience, but not one to cause me to quit running.

- I experienced pain, but in time the pain went away, and the healing began.

- I was discouraged, yes . . . defeated, no.

- The events of that day—just the events of another day in our journey.

That's where we find ourselves today. Wednesday's CT scans revealed that the chemo regimen is not working against the tumors in my shoulder and lungs. Not what we'd hoped for, and yes, we find ourselves a bit discouraged *today*. But we also know that this is only one day in our journey, another bump in the road, another obstacle to go around. So discouraged, yes, but not defeated. My oncologist here in Memphis is conferring with my team at MDA, and we hope to hear from them in a few days regarding next steps. As we know more, I'll share it with you. Until then . . .

Keep walking—even though you may have to limp.

Have I not commanded you? Be strong and courageous. Do not be afraid; do not be discouraged, for the Lord your God will be with you wherever you go. (Joshua 1:9)

Thanks for walking with me today!

CARINGBRIDGE® JOURNAL ENTRY #38
AUGUST 9, 2016

WALKING DIRECTIONALLY CHALLENGED

O K, which way do I go? If you are running a marathon or a half where both events share the same course, somewhere between miles twelve and thirteen there are signs pointing you to the direction you should go. After all, you have a decision to make. If you are running the half marathon (*only* 13.1 miles), then you are elated with the thought that the finish line is nearing, and you are so thankful that the organizers realized that your numb brain has been telling you to just mindlessly follow everybody else for the last twelve miles, and it now has a decision to make.

On the other hand, if you are participating in the full marathon, then you have another 13.1-plus miles to go. You can bask in the moment that you are halfway there before reality hits and you acknowledge that you still have the same distance to do over again. To you, that may seem an easy decision to make, but life choices are not quite so black and white.

A bad choice at this juncture and you can end up very far from where you intended. My mind recalls a *Road Runner* cartoon from childhood, where a road sign that pointed the direction ahead was changed in front of Wile E. Coyote and the image of him following that sign off the edge of a cliff to certain demise time, after time, after time (BEEP, BEEP!). As a patient fighting cancer, it often seems like there is someone out ahead of you changing those directional signs: this diagnosis then another one, this treatment then that one, surgery . . . no, wait . . . yes, let's do this clinical trial . . . well, no . . . you don't qualify after all.

A week ago, I met with another brilliant oncologist MD/ PhD to discuss participation in a local clinical trial for a promising new immunotherapy drug. It was a phase three trial that is being conducted worldwide in some 196 clinical locations involving around 720 other patients like myself. As with each clinical trial, there are a plethora of conditions that must be met for the participants and a battery of forms to be completed just to give your legal consent. Having exhausted most other options, I was eager to sign up and get underway, but the doctor said that the protocol of the trial required delaying the signature of consent for one week to allow the patient ample time to digest the forty-page Study Subject Information and Consent Form (which they sent home with me for thorough reading) and to return one week later with any questions before signing. I was scheduled to meet with her and sign the consent tomorrow at 12:30 p.m.

This morning I had a phone conversation with my oncologist back at MDA to apprise him of both my current condition and to discuss the trial. He concurred that this seemed to be my best option and said that he would speak with my local oncologist and the trial's lead investigator to echo his support of this direction.

An hour and a half later, my local oncologist called. I assumed he was calling confirming that he and the one in Houston had spoken. And he was.

"Mark, I've got some disappointing news. You didn't pass the screening for the clinical trial, and you can't participate in the trial." (There they go, changing the directional signs again!) But before my spirits could plummet, he continued. "The good news is that the FDA gave approval last Friday afternoon for an immunotherapy drug for head and neck cancers such as yours that is already showing promising results on lung cancer and melanoma. You'll be able to start on that real soon. We are also going to schedule surgery to have that lesion on your shoulder removed."

When I could use my phone, I quickly searched the Internet for news to confirm this was real. And it is! While I was sleeping this morning at 5:35 a.m., Merck issued a press release confirming that Keytruda had been approved for the treatment of head and neck squamous cell cancer. Is it a silver bullet that will take out this dreadful disease? It's too early to tell. But from my perspective, I'm looking at it as just another miracle along my journey.

Isn't it amazing how God always shows up in our time of deepest need? Or should I say, that we notice that He is there in our time of deepest need . . . because He never leaves us. This morning I felt as if our God was saying, *Well, here's your sign!*

> *Direct my footsteps according to your word; let no sin rule over me. (Psalm 119:133)*

Thanks for walking with me today!

CARINGBRIDGE® JOURNAL ENTRY #39
SEPTEMBER 1, 2016

WALKING ON A BALANCE BEAM

Our journey leads us to another surgery tomorrow (Friday, September 2) here in Memphis. Unlike the twelve-hour one I experienced thirteen months ago at MDA, this one should be relatively simple. If all goes as planned, it will be a thirty- to forty-five-minute procedure to remove the lesion on my shoulder blade, which has served as a constant reminder of my unwelcomed guest since I discovered the cancer's recurrence about five months ago. Barring any difficulty, I'll be released after surgery to come home, so I am encouraged that this can be accomplished with a "simple" day surgery instead of a not-so-simple day-long surgery as before.

The excised tissue will be sent off for genomic testing, the results of which we won't see for a month. Meanwhile, the plan is to begin the immunotherapy drug Keytruda that has just been approved by the FDA for treatment of the family of cancer that I have. They've seen encouraging results from use of this drug to help an immune system fight melanoma and lung cancer, and more recently the clinical trials for head and neck cancer showed enough promise that the FDA granted an accelerated approval for the drug to be used there as well. The treatment will be by infusion, lasting about thirty minutes every three weeks and administered at The West Clinic here in Germantown.

Is it just me, or do you see God's hand at work here? Five months ago I was, from all indications, on the road to total recovery. Then a small knot appeared on the margin of my shoulder blade. That is not so strange, but what is unusual is that I would find or even notice it. That event led to additional tests at MDA, which otherwise would not have been performed, and my recurrence would have gone undetected, and that third quarterly exam would have yielded results similar to the first two: all clear. But instead, those extra tests revealed a new demon was at work in that spot and others in my lungs and more radical chemotherapy was called for.

After managing those toxic drugs, and when that regimen failed to achieve the desired results, the doctors resorted to a phase three clinical trial that might help. Then, after being denied participation in the trial and what appeared to be the only remaining option, out of nowhere, unexpectedly, perhaps years ahead of normal FDA approval processes, this new immunotherapy drug becomes available. WOW! Tell me that He is not miraculously involved in the everydayness of our lives!

Our oldest granddaughter, Mary Collins (age six), has just begun gymnastics, and I have enjoyed watching her overcome some of her fears in the early learning sessions on the balance beam. It's new for her—something that she has never done before. From seeing her tiny, petite body awkwardly climb up to straddle the beam while holding on to it with a death grip, to her crouching while still holding fast, to then managing to boldly stand upright while wobbling uncontrollably as she looks down with apprehension at the floor below. To steady herself and achieve balance, the instructor tells her to raise her arms to shoulder height. Like the man walking the tight rope at the circus, let your arms be that pole that he uses to provide balance. Then, taking one of those hands, the instructor gently and reassuringly guides her down the length of the beam— one foot slowly in front of the other while never letting go of that hand of support. Then of course the dismount and the victorious raising of arms in achievement worthy of a gold medal. And then once on the floor, it starts all over again! Back to the other end of the beam, climb up, stand up, head up, eyes up, arms up, one foot in front of the other, dismount, ta da! Then again, and again, and again, and with each pass, the awkwardness gives way to polish, the fear subsides as confidence grows—not in perfection, mind you, but with progress and improvement. Gradually the instructor steps away . . . still present, but from a distance.

These days, I find myself on a balance beam of my own. It's called immunotherapy and it's new to me. With uncertainty I mount the beam, and my eyes immediately focus below me on the distance that I could fall. Standing there paralyzed in fear, the slightest wrong move could result in failure. With determination I position my torso upright like a statue, arms to my side. If I could just stay here frozen in the moment, I'll be fine. But no, we didn't mount the beam to be comfortable with where we are but rather to conquer it. In concert, my back foot swings forward as my arms are raised as if poised to take flight. Unstable, I start to wobble . . . but it is then that I realize that I have you to hold my hand and provide my support, and, should I fail, I have my Savior standing by to catch me when I fall. Keeping our heads up and our eyes focused not on what lies below but what is ahead. Step by step, together we will make it to the end of the beam. *And you just wait for my dismount!*

Thanks for walking with me today!

CARINGBRIDGE® JOURNAL ENTRY #40
SEPTEMBER 29, 2016

WALKING WITH MEMORIES

W hat is it with this cancer? It seems to be everywhere I turn. Family, dear friends and loved ones, work associates, fellow church members . . . the record of those smitten with this dreaded disease goes on and on. It seems as though every list of prayer requests that I see is filled with needs related either to those suffering with the illness in its many forms or for their caregivers. And the lists seem to grow and spread like the cancer itself.

She would have been one hundred years old this month, had she lived. Cora Lee Raley (Wiggins) was born on September 12, 1916, to a humble couple in rural South Alabama. She was their first child but would grow to be sibling and mentor to four younger sisters and one younger brother. She grew to be the kind of example you want for your kids, particularly the oldest as she would literally help raise her sisters and brother. Those responsibilities would mean that she'd never complete high school, but the education in life that she earned would far surpass an institutional degree. She would eventually marry and carry those traits into her marriage. And yes, I am fortunate to have called her my mother!

Growing up in those demanding years did much to shape her character. As an infant, she would have experienced the impact of World War I. Her teenage years would have brought the uncertainty of an economy ravaged by the first Wall Street crash and the economic depression that followed. For many years, polio was a constant threat. The next decade would usher in yet another war, and this time family members would respond to the call to serve their country. All of a sudden, battles on foreign soil to defend and preserve freedom of those she would never know became far too personal. It was during these years (1945, 1950, and 1955) that she would introduce three children into this uncertain world, and, unfortunately, things did little to improve. Nuclear armament ushered in the Cuban Missile Crisis of the early sixties, the Civil Rights Movement added racial strife, and the unthinkable assassinations of President John F. Kennedy, Senator Robert Kennedy, and Martin Luther King Jr. all left us wondering, *What is going on?*

Perhaps it is because of all of this that the woman that I saw in her never seemed to be rattled in the face of all of the uncertainty and adversity that I grew up with. When you add it all up, by the time that I showed up in her life, she'd pretty well faced it all. Even when she received her diagnosis of breast cancer in 1968, she took it in stride and continued her mission. Although through my teenage years, I would witness the intense pain and suffering that the next five years would bring her, those memories are medicated for me by far better memories.

Among the many things I remember are,

1. *Her willingness to teach me* as we slaved side by side in an intensely hot kitchen, where I learned the basics of cooking (which I still enjoy to this day). I never remember her not having time to answer my endless questions.

2. *Learning appreciation of God's creation* as we walked barefoot through the damp morning grass and into the dusty tilled soil, hand in hand with parents that both loved me and valued me.

3. *Learning to be thorough* as we inched along in rows side by side in the pea patch (the garden, for you Yankees) behind

our home. She turned a routine chore into an art form by helping me to understand that not all of the pods are ready to be picked yet, just as a young boy sometimes is not ready to do the things his older brother and sister could do.

4. *Learning to be patient* . . . as the seemingly endless row of peas was completed, you now turn around and pick two rows back to the house . . . but this time, butter beans! If you have never had a picking experience, you have no idea of the painful emotion in that last sentence.

5. *Learning commitment* when said peas and beans were then shelled by hand and blanched and cooled before placed in bags and into the freezer for consumption in the months ahead.

6. *Learning to have pride* because of what we had accomplished through hard work . . . together.

7. *Learning to be disciplined* . . . when she beat the snot out of me with Bridal Wreath whenever I would *misbehave*—a seemingly broad and sometimes all-encompassing term for whatever I happened to be doing wrong at the time. For those of you who don't know, Bridal Wreath is an indigenous South Alabama shrub likened to the ancient Cat of Nine Tails when stripped of their leaves. Forget choosing your own, because I quickly learned that, large or small, each wreaked its own unique havoc on bare legs and bottoms. Should verbal outburst ensue, said discipline above could be followed with my mouth being "washed out" with soap. Dial soap was the family standard, and the few times that I needed reminding, I never acquired the taste for it.

I don't remember the expensive vacations we didn't go on, the fine house that we didn't live in, the fancy cars that were "entitled" of me. I do remember some of the things we did without but nothing that was really important that we didn't have. Memories—they're what remain and, in many ways, what make us.

My wife, Lesa, has a special place. It's a place where I find her every morning when I awaken. It's beside . . . *a wine crate*. Now, while living with me can certainly drive one to drinking, it was already empty the day she fetched it from outside a local liquor store. Although I typically rise around 7:00 a.m. (What? *I am* retired, you know!), she has often been sitting there for up to two hours before me with Bible open, eyes swollen from tears shed through prayer, and faithfully chronicling in her journal the days of this journey we are sharing together. She has converted the empty wine box to her own Ark of the Covenant. You know the one I'm talking about— the holy "box" that God instructed Moses to build to illustrate God going before the children of Israel on their wilderness journey and that He was not only constantly with them but constantly leading them in what seemed to be an endless nomadic walk through the desert. As with Moses, Lesa's "ark/box" contains God's Word of instruction to us, along with a collection of valued devotional guides, pens, highlighters, and markers.

But rather than being adorned with gold, she has instead chosen to pen scriptures of God's promises that we have selected to hold onto for *our* journey. It started with one verse, but the box is rapidly running out of space. The best example I know of "thinking outside the box!" Also included there are quotes and sayings from famous writers, theologians, and others. It's amazing to see so many truths and promises captured there as a reminder of God's faithfulness and goodness to His children.

I've walked you a long way today to reach my point. My mother's life here on this earth was a mere fifty-eight years, yet she impacted it for God's good more than many who live to be one hundred. One of the quotes on Lesa's ark is from Steve Turley. It's simple, yet I find it quite profound:

One day you will just be a memory to someone. Make it a good one!

Oh yeah, you were expecting an update!

One of the things that I have learned in communicating on CaringBridge® over the last seventeen months is that people assume that no news is bad news, and oftentimes that is the case.

Not here . . . not now. The last three weeks since my last post have not been bad, just busy.

The surgery to remove the lesion from my shoulder went well. Stitches are out, and healing is great. The biopsy of that tissue was consistent with the other cancer biopsies, so good news is that nothing different has cropped up. The remaining tissue was sent to Foundation One for genomic testing, and we are still awaiting those findings. Meanwhile, on the Wednesday following surgery, I began Keytruda immunotherapy. I was sailing along beautifully with no apparent side effects until about ten days in, at which point I began having issues with double vision. It gradually got worse over the next four days so that I had to stop driving. I can see fine out of either eye independently, but my binocular vision is off. This week I saw a couple of specialists, and they think it may be a side effect of the Keytruda. So . . . cycle two, which was to be administered today, has been delayed until the eye issue clears up. I began steroids today, which hopefully will remedy it. Until then, I get to continue enjoying seeing twice as much of each new day. God is so good!

Just another bump in the road!

Thanks for walking with me today!

CARINGBRIDGE® JOURNAL ENTRY #41
OCTOBER 15, 2016

WALKING . . . INTO A BLIND CURVE

W e recognized a significant milestone in our journey this past week. It was the one-year celebration of our homecoming journey back from MDA in Houston. In late September of 2015, and with the helpful assistance of our friends Randy and Betsy McKinney, the Eagle motor coach began its long trek back to Memphis after having spent five months in Houston as our base camp for diagnosis, surgery, and treatment. We broke the trip into three manageable segments, arriving in Auburn, Alabama, for a football game weekend and a much-needed time to recharge our batteries before continuing on the final leg into Memphis. Although it was the plan that I had asked for, I was in no shape to go to a ball game. While Randy had capably piloted the rig to its new home for the rest of the season, I was physically drained from the chemo and radiation that had concluded the week before. So, while so thankful to be back in a familiar, happy place, I was content to just rest as we prepared to face the recovery that lies ahead.

But oh, what a difference a year makes! This year I was actually able to enjoy not only the game but also my family and friends that surrounded me. This year was totally different—back to more of a norm, albeit a new normal. Energy reserves were greatly improved, and if not for the double vision issues, I'd say that things were definitely headed in the right direction.

After enjoying a great Auburn homecoming football victory, we were allowed to go onto the field at Jordan Hare Stadium. It was my first opportunity to do so, and what a treat and what a change of perspective to be on the inside looking out. Gazing up at the endless rows of seats, they appeared to be canyon walls reaching into the late afternoon sky. I stood at the fifty-yard line and made a quick three-hundred-sixty-degree mental panoramic impression. One feels so small and insignificant as you get lost in the enormity of it all. Joined there by probably a couple thousand other fans, I was strangely touched that this is a picture of what the sea of people that have prayed for me over the last eighteen months would look like. Many of the faces would be as unrecognizable as were those fans that I was struggling to keep from stepping on. It must be terribly exciting to play on this field of conquest, but I was overwhelmed more by a moment of gratitude and appreciation for those who have, and continue to, lift me up in prayer.

Returning to Memphis, I met for my weekly consult with the oncologist. It was then that the road unexpectedly veered into a blind curve.

"Forget what we told you last week. The diplopia (double vision) is not being caused by your immunotherapy drug, so the good news is that we can start you back on that tomorrow. The bad news is that you have another tumor located where your optic nerve comes out of your brain (not in your brain) and goes to that eye. So we are going to need to get some radiation treatment for that."

So I await my consult with the neurosurgeon next Wednesday. It appears that I will have a gamma knife procedure, which hopefully can eradicate that spot, putting an end to this latest recurrence and hopefully restoring my vision to normalcy.

I leave you today with this poem from a favorite writer of mine from the 80s. It was good then and is even better today:

Someday I'll, by Denis Waitley

There is an island fantasy
Called "Someday I'll" (we'll never see)
Where recession stops, inflation ceases
Our mortgage is paid and our pay increases

That Someday I'll where problems end
Where every piece of mail is from a friend
And the children are sweet (and already grown!)
And all the other nations can go it alone

Where we all retire at forty-one
Playing backgammon in the island sun

Most unhappy people look to tomorrow
To erase this day of hardship and sorrow
They put happiness on lay-away
And struggle through another blue today

But happiness cannot be sought
It can't be earned, it can't be bought
Life's most important revelation
It's the journey that counts . . . not just the destination

Happiness . . . is where you are right now
It's pushing a pencil or pushing a plow
It's going to school or standing in line
It's watching and waiting, or tasting the wine
It's knocking on doors and making your calls
It's getting back up after your falls

If you live in the past you become senile
If you live in the future . . . you're on Someday I'll

The fear of results is procrastination
The joy of today is a celebration
You can save, you can slave, trudging mile after mile
But you'll never set foot on your Someday I'll

When you've paid all your dues and put in your time
Out of nowhere comes another Mt. Everest to climb
So from this day forward make it your vow
Take Someday I'll and make it . . . NOW [5]

Rather than being a spectator in life, get out of the stands and onto the field. Your perspective will be forever changed!

Thanks for walking with me today!

---

5. Denis Waitley, *Seeds of Greatness* (New Jersey: Fleming H. Revell Company, 1983), 213-214. "Someday I'll," printed with permission from the author.

CARINGBRIDGE® JOURNAL ENTRY #42
NOVEMBER 17, 2016

WALKING WITH A GAMMA KNIFE

I t was like a scene from a 1960s science fiction thriller—the only exception being seen in color rather than black and white. With my right eye occluded by a patch, vision in my left eye was like looking down a pipe: only adding to the special effects.

"OK, Mr. Wiggins," the nurse began. "We are going to mount the frame to your head now. We're going to give you lidocaine injections in four places around your head, so this will sting but only for a moment." She was right.

The doctor had stepped into my frame of view. "This will be uncomfortable, but only for about thirty seconds. I'm going to screw the frame into your head in four places. You'll just feel pressure more than anything else. Once we begin, I'll proceed as quickly as I can to get them all done. Ready?"

I rendered my agreement to proceed, the last time for the next six hours that I would have a say in anything. The two nurses held the titanium halo in position as the doctor methodically and precisely drilled the screws one by one into their stabilizing positions. Yep, it sounded just like a drill from a construction site or an auto repair shop; only the fasteners were being firmly implanted in my skull.

With my new stabilizing partner onboard, I was escorted to the MRI suite for an updated scan. This would provide the latest status on the position, size, and involvement of the tumor that is also affecting my optic nerve and resulting in vision issues. It would also provide the 3D data feed into the gamma knife, from which the radiation dosage and path plan would be administered.

Ten minutes later, I was fitted with a special helmet with 201 ports, which would beam and focus radiation into a single pinpoint. That helmet was also precisely designed to fit into the gamma knife's motorized gurney, ensuring that it would be locked into position upon demand.

As I was laying on the gurney before the procedure started, the radiological physicist cautioned that we were in for a long day. While the MRI revealed that the tumor had not grown, and no additional lesions were detected, its location and proximity to important nerves required a strategic approach with the beam. She said we were looking at probably sixteen or so passes and encouraged me to relax and sleep as much as I could, which would be my main priority considering the happy meds that were already having their effects on me.

She must have pushed more meds as she moved me into the gamma knife tunnel because for the next four and a half hours, I was resting in deep sleep. I was actually annoyed when they intentionally roused me to check on how I was doing with an hour and a half left on the procedure. But they did tell me that it was OK to reposition my lower body and extremities at will if needed, realizing that I had been laying in the same position for over six hours. It was a relief to stretch and bend and even move my knees up to my waist, but one thing was certain: my head was not moving except for where they wanted it to go.

Now marginally awake, I began noting the regular pattern of events going on around me. A pleasant, melodious alarm would play, indicating we were about to go into the next cycle. Then the gurney would move my body back into the tube. The faint whir of servo motors began as they adjusted my head to the next position to be treated. Then a jarring sound and feeling as the mechanism locked into position. Then a pleasant tone beeped throughout the duration of that pass. Once done, it all repeated.

It was during this time that I was particularly impressed by how little control I had over my head. Actually, it was *none*. I remember consciously trying to will my head to go in opposition to where the motors were taking it, but there was no chance of that happening. The doctors and those that designed this marvelous device knew how critical it was to allow no margin for error, and the pin-point accuracy and precision with which the radiation was delivered would yield great results . . . as long as my head was in the right place!

That was two weeks ago. Outside of the lingering effects from the anesthesia meds, which have destroyed my appetite and rendered a prevailing nausea, the procedure was a nonevent. No new pain and even some signs of relief, although the final results are still weeks away. In the days since that gamma knife procedure, I have been struck by the teachings of this procedure for me.

I thought of how that instrument, with the aid of its skilled doctors and physicists, knew exactly where to focus the radiation to kill cancerous cells while avoiding damage to surrounding tissues. How it willfully positioned my head to receive the radiation dosage. How it securely maintained that position as long as was needed before moving on to the next group of coordinates. How it knew when it was done and ready to then move to another angle of attack. How, when I relinquished my will to the will of the machine, it not only knew the path to take but it also knew the treatment plan to get the desired results.

Although it pales in comparison, isn't that the way it looks when we turn over *our will* and instead seek *God's will* for our lives? We don't know the direction, and so we cannot see the destination. When we seek *His will*, it is like having that frame mounted to our heads, ensuring that we don't stray off on our own while keeping our focus on *His* plan and our eyes ready to see *Him* at work in the playing out of the details. All the while, He *securely* keeps us moving along through our journey, avoiding obstacles and inconveniences, or merely annihilating them with a power far greater than 201 beams of focused gamma radiation. Simply *amazing*!

For those of you keeping up with my journey, yesterday I received round four of Keytruda immunotherapy treatment. Next up is a scan on December 7 to determine its effectiveness. We covet your prayers in the days ahead and for good results . . . in keeping with *God's will*.

Thanks for walking with me today!

CARINGBRIDGE® JOURNAL ENTRY #43
DECEMBER 1, 2016

WALKING IN THANKSGIVING

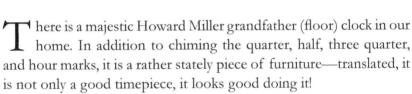

There is a majestic Howard Miller grandfather (floor) clock in our home. In addition to chiming the quarter, half, three quarter, and hour marks, it is a rather stately piece of furniture—translated, it is not only a good timepiece, it looks good doing it!

At the heart of every floor clock is the movement. The movement controls the hour strike, time keeping, and chime. The pendulum and weights are critical components to operation of the clock movement. The pendulum provides the ability to regulate and adjust the time keeping. The three weights provide power to the hour strike (left weight), time (center weight), and chime melody (right weight). Without these weights, the clock would not operate. Each weight is different and must be properly hung from the movement (left, center, and right) to ensure proper operation.

Now that I am in retirement, one of my "chores" is to pause at least once every seven days to wind the clock. Otherwise, it ceases to function as a timepiece as it was destined to do and is left just looking pretty. After I have cranked the weights to their position, I pause to say a quick prayer of thanksgiving for the week that has successfully passed and that I now view out my rear-view mirror. I also ask to be granted another week to finish my work here, whatever that may be.

Winding the clock serves as a reminder to me of the fragility of life and how precious each day has become and how each of us must live it to the fullest. Someone once said that children spell love, T-I-M-E. I've grown to be convinced that is true, whatever the age of your children.

It also reminds me that to achieve the desired results (accurate timekeeping), the components must act together in harmony. The same is true for us. Whether it be family, a young couple starting a marriage together, a sports team, or a business, working together is the only way to get the desired results. This means that each individual is responsible for pulling their own share of the load. Just like the three weights in that clock have unique design and purpose, so do each of us.

I continue to feel better with each passing day. Appetite is back, and I'm looking forward to a clean scan next Wednesday, December 7. Please continue to pray with me. Miracles are happening all around me. Thank you once again.

Take time to count your blessings this Thanksgiving season. Claim every new day as your own Thanksgiving Day.

Give thanks to the Lord of lords: His love endures forever. (Psalm 136:3)

Thanks for walking with me today!

CARINGBRIDGE® JOURNAL ENTRY #44
JANUARY 6, 2017

WALKING IN DISAPPOINTMENT

I t had been the appointment that I'd truly looked forward to. Four Keytruda treatments had passed, and the MRI would hopefully reveal that this immunotherapy regimen would finally enable my body to take control of fighting the disease. I'd felt noticeably better overall, and if not for the double-vision that continued to plague my every move, I felt . . . well, normal.

That was four weeks ago now. The disappointing news was that it appears the immunotherapy path is not working; my cancer continues to stump the experts. The scan showed that the couple of small tumors in my lungs had grown by twenty-five percent while others that were barely noticeable before were now the size of pencil points. There was an outside chance that the Keytruda could be causing them to inflame and appear to have grown before visibly beginning to shrink and be under control. The good news is that they are small and appear to be growing slowly. So, after additional consults, I am undergoing a couple more Keytruda infusions (one more now) and then having an additional scan.

And then there's the brain tumor and the results of the gamma knife procedure. I'm still six weeks away from that follow-up visit.

Although I have already sensed some tactile improvements, impaired vision is still a constant, debilitating companion.

It never ceases to amaze me how our Creator fashioned us with the utmost of fascinating detail . . . things that we all take for granted each day. Among them is how He blessed us with binocular vision rather than giving us just one eye. Could we get by with just one? Well, yes, but He chose instead to give us the bonus of using one eye to complement the other and to achieve a greater amount of focus and detail. Having two eyes working in concert perfects both depth perception and the ability to see a wide and panoramic array of objects without having to turn our heads. Two eyes in harmony gives one the ability to have peripheral vision, which allows us to fully see objects entering that field of vision and signals the brain to make the appropriate response. And of course, balance. Being deprived of a correctly functioning right eye is like transforming a svelte ballet dancer to a bumbling, stumbling fool. Careful, here I come!

These days I'm frequently reminded of my mother's warning as a child: "Stop crossing your eyes, they'll get stuck that way!" Or of the character Ruby Sue in the movie *Christmas Vacation* who, according to her dad, Cousin Eddie, "falls in a well and her eyes cross and then gets kicked by a mule and they go back to normal . . . I don't know!"

So we are disappointed but not disillusioned! Our God is faithful to deliver healing according to His timing. We've just finished celebrating a great holiday season that spanned Thanksgiving, Christmas, and New Year's—celebrations that eighteen months ago were forecasted to be far different. I've been reminded afresh that it was not about the *presents* but the *presence*—presence of family, presence of friends, and presence of the Holy Spirit who gives us His peace.

Just as He gives us more than we need with regard to our vision, He gives us good gifts—more than we need and certainly more than we deserve.

If you, then, though you are evil, know how to give good gifts to your children, how much more will your Father in heaven give good gifts to those who ask him! (Matthew 7:11)

Thanks for walking with me today!

CARINGBRIDGE® JOURNAL ENTRY #45
FEBRUARY 5, 2017

WALKING . . . IN SEARCH OF MIRACLES

I see so much of my three-year-old granddaughter coming out in me: needy and impatient! These days I quite often find myself wanting so much more and wanting it right now! It's frustrating when you serve a God so great that is so capable of meeting your every need but seems to be silent. But then again, the truth is, it is more likely that He is still actively at work on making me more dependent on Him and less on myself or the medicine or the doctors.

This week's CT scans showed mixed results. On the one hand, many of the lung nodules were stable, while others that were pinpoint in size had grown. Of the three that are being most closely monitored, two showed no growth, while one had grown a little. And there was no new growth. So the assessment now is that perhaps the immunotherapy drug is slowing the progress of the cancer, and the plan at this point is to continue with three more treatments and to scan again in nine weeks.

Good news takeaways from this week's visit are that we may be slowing the growth and that there are still many unknowns as to how the Keytruda impacts the kind of cancer I have due both to its recent approval for use on head and neck and lung cancer and due to the rare cancer I have. It could just need more infusions and more time. So we keep up the regimen and wait.

The following was published by Mark Batterson on September 19, 2014, on FoxNews.com, on the subject of miracles. It merits a few moments to read:

> *I know people who say they have never experienced a miracle. Maybe you're one of them. But I would argue that you have never not experienced one.*
>
> *It may seem like you're sitting still right now, but it's an illusion of miraculous proportions. Planet Earth is spinning around its axis at an equatorial speed of 1,040 miles per hour.*
>
> *Simultaneously, we're also speeding through space at an average velocity of 67,108 miles per hour. That's not just faster than a speeding bullet. It's eighty-seven times faster than the speed of sound.*
>
> *So even on a day when you feel like you didn't get much done, you did travel 1,599,793 miles through space! And to top things off, the Milky Way Galaxy is spinning like a top at the mind-boggling rate of 483,000 mph.*
>
> *If that isn't miraculous, I don't know what is.*
>
> *Yet when was the last time you thanked God for keeping us in orbit? I'm guessing never! "Lord, I wasn't sure we'd make the full rotation today, but You did it again!"*
>
> *We just don't pray that way. Why? Because God is so good at what He does that we take it for granted. Now here's my point. You already believe God for the big miracles like they're no big deal. The trick is learning to trust Him for the little ones.*
>
> *Albert Einstein said, "There are only two ways to live your life. One is as if nothing is a miracle. The other as if everything is."*
>
> *I unapologetically believe that everything is.*

Trillions of chemical reactions are taking place in your body every second of every day—you are inhaling oxygen, metabolizing energy, managing equilibrium, manufacturing hormones, fighting antigens, filtering stimuli, purifying toxins, and circulating six quarts of blood through 60,000 miles of arteries, veins, and capillaries. If the blood vessels in your body were laid end to end, they'd circle the earth two and a half times!

Your brain has the ability to perform ten quadrillion calculations per second using only twenty watts of power. And its storage capacity is 2.5 petabytes. The entire print collection of the Library of Congress is estimated to be 10 terabytes. So your brain has the capacity to store 250 libraries of congress.

If your personal genome sequence were written out longhand, it would be a three-billion-word book. The King James Version has 783,137 words, so your genetic code is the equivalent of approximately four thousand Bibles. If your personal genome sequence were an audio book, and you were to read at the rate of one double helix per second, it would take nearly a century to put you into words!

My point? You aren't just surrounded by miracles. You are one.

What if we started living like it? How would it change our daily lives? How would it change the way we treat the walking, talking, miracles we live with and work with each day?

One last miracle.

You will take approximately 23,000 breaths today. As a life-long asthmatic, I don't take them for granted. Each one is the miracle of life. We'd be a lot happier, healthier, and holier if we thanked God for each one.[6]

I think Mr. Batterson summed it up pretty well. If my God spoke the miracle of life into order and maintains the universe, then

---

6. Mark Batterson, FoxNews.com (2014). http://www.foxnews.com/opinion/2014/09/19/arent-just-surrounded-by-miracles-are-one.html. Used with permission from the author.

He's got my cancer along with whatever miracle it is that you are in need of today.

> *I will lift up mine eyes unto the hills, from whence cometh my help. My help cometh from the Lord, which made heaven and earth. He will not suffer thy foot to be moved: he that keepeth thee will not slumber. Behold, he that keepeth Israel shall neither slumber nor sleep. (Psalm 121:1-4 KJV)*

Thanks for walking with me today!

CARINGBRIDGE® JOURNAL ENTRY #46
APRIL 11, 2017

WALKING FOR A SECOND

Life can change in a second. It could come in the form of a shocking cancer diagnosis (or recurrence), a tragic automobile accident, a simple tree-trimming chore ending horribly wrong, a late-term pregnancy gone awry, disappointing reality that a marriage is finally, painfully over. All of life's plans, all of your personal goals, all of the places you wanted to go and things you wanted to do, all of the experiences you'd hoped to share . . . can come to a radical halt in just a second. I've always lived by the mantra to "prepare as if you were going to live forever, but live as though today was your last." After all, each day is indeed a gift. But sometimes, regardless of how well you prepare and how hard you work, and plan, and set those goals, and develop a life-plan to get there . . . it all changes in a second.

It was November 30, 2013. A typical hard-fought Iron Bowl football classic was moments away from going into overtime as the final seconds of regulation play were ticking down. The Alabama Crimson Tide topped the preseason rankings at number one and were only two wins away from claiming a third straight BCS title.

But they found themselves tied 28-28 with a tenacious Auburn team who had surprisingly ascended to the number four spot in the BCS rankings. Alabama had both possession of the ball and the momentum and was driving, but their player stepped out of bounds just as the clock ticked to zero. An official review would reveal there was 0:01 left with the ball on the Auburn thirty-nine-yard line when his foot touched down . . . just time enough for a hail Mary pass into the end zone for a win or, could it be, a game-winning field goal that would be a record fifty-seven yarder. Coach Nick Saban elected to go with the field goal. After all, a miss would mean overtime, and he must have been secure in the fact that his undefeated team would win that battle.

But then the impossible happened: snap down, kick off, sailing on its way toward the Auburn goalpost. For a moment, it looked like it may make it, but the ball faded to the right and short of the goal and into the waiting arms of Auburn's number eleven, Chris Davis. He sprinted toward the center of the field for about fifteen yards and then veered sharply to the left, picking up the wall of Auburn teammates that formed while everyone else had been gazing skyward.

From my seat on the fifty-yard line, I was having difficulty processing what I was seeing. Having watched college football religiously for over five decades, I had never seen what I was witnessing being played out in front of me. Davis continued, sprinting up the Auburn sideline, and was joined by a couple of other teammates, escorting him to the goal line. *Please don't touch him, please don't fall down, please don't do anything stupid,* I thought. And none of those happened. I quickly scanned the field for penalty flags that would thwart the victory, and I saw none. It was history . . . game over . . . *all* because of 0:01!

A cornerstone of successful football programs is goal setting, and while I have never visited the University of Alabama locker room, I am confident that the team's goals are prominently displayed so that the players are clearly and constantly reminded of the expectations that everyone is working toward. It would look something like this:

Goal #1—Win the National Championship
Goal #2—Have an Undefeated Season
Goal #3—Win the SEC Championship
Goal #4—Win the SEC Western Division
Goal #5—Beat Auburn in the Iron Bowl
Etc., etc., etc.

As they made their way to the locker room, the gravity of that one second would begin to soak in for the Alabama team. It was a costly and devastating one second. There must have been some point that their minds reflected back to those goals.

Goal #1—Win the National Championship (*lost in a second*)
Goal #2—Have an Undefeated Season (*lost in a second*)
Goal #3—Win the SEC Championship (*lost in a second*)
Goal #4—Win the SEC Western Division (*lost in a second*)
Goal #5—Beat Auburn in the Iron Bowl (*lost in a second*)

How would you be prepared to face a life-changing second? We all have an appointment with one . . .

When you pass through the waters, I will be with you; and when you pass through the rivers, they will not sweep over you. When you walk through the fire, you will not be burned; the flames will not set you ablaze. For I am the Lord your God, the Holy One of Israel, your Savior. (Isaiah 43:2-3a)

Last week our journey reached yet another uphill obstacle. While it was thought that the Keytruda immunotherapy had slowed the cancer somewhat, new scans showed additional growth. My doctors have ordered up a new chemotherapy twenty-one-day regimen that I started yesterday. I'll have a heavy dose of drugs on Monday of the first week, only one of the two drugs the following Monday, no drugs on the third Monday, and then it repeats all over again. I will have progress scans after two cycles (six weeks).

There aren't any new side effects that I have to look forward to that I had not been warned about in previous chemo protocols, so I hope that I can manage these as well as I did the previous ones. They say that I can bank on hair loss, but what the heck; summer's almost here, so I am ready for a low maintenance alternative, and that one's hard to beat.

Thank you for walking with me today.

CARINGBRIDGE® JOURNAL ENTRY #47
AUGUST 16, 2017

WALKING . . . WITH HOPE!

I did a little reminiscing today.

It was my last appointment at MDA: May 4, 2016. We'd received the disappointing news of the recurrence of my cancer, this time in new locations presenting new challenges. The medical oncologist recited the sobering news once more: "You have a very rare cancer, there is no known cure for it, your treatment plan going forward will be palliative care (trying to make the best of the time you have left). We're sending you home where they can administer the recommended chemotherapy, which is a very strong combination of three drugs. But I have to tell you that if this doesn't work, you are looking at six months to live." It seemed as if I had just been issued my death sentence.

That was sixteen months ago. And no, those heavy rounds of chemo did not work. The hopeful immunotherapy drug, Keytruda, failed to deliver as well. A switch to a sarcoma-focused chemo treatment plan of Doxorubicin and Lartruvo had shown no marked improvement . . . until yesterday. Wait, yes . . . I said *improvement*! The news from yesterday's scan: no growth in lung tumors, and several had decreased in size by ten to twenty percent. This means that apparently this latest chemo effort is having an effect of at least stabilizing progression. Finally, some good news!

But wait, there's more. On Monday, I had my quarterly follow up with the neurologist regarding my optic nerve tumor. The MRI there revealed a perfectly normal scan, meaning that the gamma knife procedure done last November was effective in dissolving that tumor. We even talked about a procedure that could be done in the coming months to correct my double vision, provided the body doesn't correct it on its own.

God is at work here. Though we may not have seen Him answer the petition of the moment (of which we find there are many), He is faithfully making Himself known in the many details of our lives. Cancer is a formidable adversary, and you must never lose sight of the fact that you are in the battle of your life. And as much as we'd like to get immediate results, it just doesn't happen that way. Treatments continue to evolve, and new drugs are working their way through clinical trials. To put that in perspective, Keytruda has only been approved for my type of cancer for eleven months. Lartruvo, one of my current chemo drugs, has only been on the market for use against sarcomas for ten months. A year ago, neither of those options would have been available to me.

Again, I find myself in need of apologizing for not giving you an update in several months. It seems that it has just been a repetitive exercise of clinic visits, infusions, doctor consultations, and testing that are just a part of going down this path. Oh yeah, and there was the week I spent in the hospital fighting an infection. Not a good thing when your immune system has been virtually wiped out by chemo.

But we continue in the fight, and I know that we are not fighting alone. The faithful prayers that continue to be voiced on our behalf are what has sustained us this far. You will never know how much we appreciate you standing by us and walking with us on this journey. Regardless of when we aren't seeing progress, we are continuing the fight.

In 1972 US distance runner Dave Wottle made a historic comeback to win the gold medal in the Munich Olympics. It was against all odds. The rest of the field was faster, and Dave was struggling with arthritis in his knees, which had hampered his training in the weeks coming up to the race.

He was born in 1950 in Canton, Ohio, and took up running in childhood because he was so feeble. During the 1972 Olympic games in Munich, in the eight-hundred-meter final, Wottle immediately found himself in the rear of the field and stayed there for the first five hundred meters, at which point he started to pass runner after runner up the final straight. Amazingly he seized the lead in the final stretch to beat race favorite Yevgeny Arzhanov of the Soviet Union by just 0.03 seconds, in the best eight-hundred-meter Olympic run in history! (Take a moment to find a video of this run on YouTube. Dave is wearing the golf cap and can be easily spotted all by himself at the rear of the pack for most of the race.)

Dave won an Olympic gold medal against all odds and never gave up even though the outlook for most of the race was bleak. As I made it clear to my family from the start, giving up is not an option for us.

> *Therefore, since we are surrounded by such a great cloud of witnesses, let us throw off everything that hinders and the sin that so easily entangles. And let us run with perseverance the race marked out for us. (Hebrews 12:1)*

Thanks for walking with me today!

CARINGBRIDGE® JOURNAL ENTRY #48
OCTOBER 7, 2017

WALKING . . . AND WINNING!

W inning is a wonderful thing! As a young person growing up, it didn't take me long to learn that in whatever endeavor, winning was the desired outcome. It was part of my developmental DNA—instilled by my parents and encouraged and modeled by my siblings and extended family. Whether part of a team competition or a personal quest, the expectation was to bring home a win. Being part of a successful high school football program, I learned firsthand the thrill of victory (winning) twenty-seven times while feeling the agony of defeat (losing or tying) on only five occasions. Winning became something I desired to repeat!

And rightly so . . . I'm sure that you have experienced it too. Winning brings joy, satisfaction, confidence, and a sense of accomplishment. Winning has an alluring affect about it—the almost intoxicating sensation that comes along with winning draws one to it like a moth to a flame. I'm convinced that the reason the University of Alabama has such a huge football fan base is due to its appeal to folks to identify with a winner. And rightly so; most weekends you can count on them for a win, giving fans a frequent rush of the above-mentioned benefits.

I experienced those feelings afresh this week. My latest CT scan revealed that my cancer is stable—a huge victory and a needed *win*. This means that my chemo regimen can be reduced to a maintenance drug for the foreseeable future. Tests also showed that my heart's efficiency had improved—an important marker due to the heavy-duty chemo that I'd been taking.

So we are celebrating our God's goodness in providing yet another win. I hope that you will slow down enough today to recognize His provision in your life and the many ways He offers a winning option for living life to the fullest!

I press on toward the goal to win the prize for which God has called me heavenward in Christ Jesus. (Philippians 3:14)

Thanks for walking with me today!

CARINGBRIDGE® JOURNAL ENTRY #49
DECEMBER 5, 2017

WALKING . . . IN NEED OF WATER

Water: it covers almost three fourths of the planet we inhabit. It comprises over sixty percent of an adult male's body, a delicate balance of which is essential for normal systems' maintenance and function. It's a commodity that most of us have always taken for granted.

As a child, I remember the satisfaction of taking a long drag of water from a garden hose on a scorching hot summer day. It was *free*, it was *satisfying*, and it was *abundant*. Never could I begin to comprehend then that one day I would be paying for finite amounts of this beverage that is contained in disposable plastic bottles that I tote around with me.

Water has taken on a new meaning for me throughout my various cancer treatments. Because most of my salivary glands were sacrificed in surgery, I find myself in constant need of liquids to replace their normal function. Early into treatment as the medical team gave their myriad of instructions, drinking enough water was at the top of their lists. If you don't drink enough water, then this, this, this, this, and this could happen. And I can validate that several of those have proven out as I, at times, failed to keep up with the daily regimen of taking on more fluids than I assimilated, resulting in ugly, painful, and even dangerous results and life-threatening consequences.

Today, water is my necessary, constant companion. I suffer from an insatiable thirst far worse than the "cotton mouth" you'd get from running wind sprints at the end of football practice! You will rarely find me now without a water bottle within arm's length.

And through this experience, today I better understand the thirst that comes from severe water shortage following a natural disaster, of crops and vegetation that wither and die due to drought. I can now relate to a soldier in a Middle Eastern desert who has to consciously remember to fill his or her canteen whenever possible and to carefully ration its contents throughout the mission. Water is necessary for our very survival.

Recently I stood at the ocean's door in Gulf Shores, Alabama, looking out on the flat surface of blue, thinking of the magnitude of the Gulf of Mexico. Later, from our twenty-fourth-floor condo I could begin to appreciate the vastness of just what could be seen from this heightened vantage point, gazing miles into a one hundred eighty degree spectrum while fully realizing that even this was only a small sampling of the earth's enormous water supply.

God knew the importance that water would play in our lives from day three of Creation when He separated the land from the sea. He knew the essential role that it would play in the very existence of His creation and its ability to survive and thrive. He chose this image of "living water" to communicate to us the spiritual need of His Son, Jesus. Just as we need physical water to live, we need this living water to quench our spiritual thirst. In Jesus' encounter with the Samaritan woman at Jacob's well in John chapter 4 . . .

> Jesus answered, "Everyone who drinks this water will be thirsty again, but whoever drinks the water I give them will never thirst. Indeed, the water I give them will become in them a spring of water welling up to eternal life." (John 4:13-14)

The living water He offers to each of us is *free*, it's *satisfying*, and it's *abundant*.

Yesterday I had my routine CT scans to monitor our progress in the fight against my disease. The last two scans had indicated that the cancer was stable and that treatment was being effective. Unfortunately, the most recent results were not as promising, with increases in size of several of the tumors, while others remained stable. We will continue the current treatment path for another six weeks and test again—just another bend in the road of life's journey.

Water—it's an essential component of life's walk. Don't forget to get yours today!

Thanks for walking with me today!

CARINGBRIDGE® JOURNAL ENTRY #50
JANUARY 2, 2018

WALKING . . . TO BETHLEHEM

C hristmas 2017 . . . it's now in the record books. The tree is down, and the decorations are once again stored in their attic home. It's been a blessed time of family as we had all of the kids and grandkids here with us—some for nine days!

For me, personally, it was the best Christmas ever! No, I didn't get the gift that I've always longed for (couldn't even tell you what that might be). No, we didn't go everywhere and do everything we had planned. No, I didn't eat to excess . . . enjoying the seasonal flavors of the holiday that I have always loved. Even the weather disappointed us with a wet and cold weekend. It was best because it was a gift of life that I was fortunate to receive. You see, this is the second Christmas I've celebrated where I wasn't supposed to be here. So, while we all should be thankful to wake on Christmas morning to the sounds of chaos as kids and grandkids with unbridled excitement race to see what presents they'll get, for me, it's a little more personal. It's about presence . . . not the presents!

Over the holiday, I reflected on a past Christmas of my childhood. The property of our home was next to a pasture of probably twenty acres or so that was habitation to a few head of a neighbor's cattle. As a child I remember standing one clear cold Christmas Eve looking out across that pasture, wondering what it must have been like for the shepherds that first Christmas. A brilliant full moon illuminated the night sky for me, lighting up the landscape in clear detail. There were no sheep that night but rather a few cows and their calves. The quiet stillness was sporadically interrupted by the distant painful bellowing of a cow (which I later learned was giving birth to a new calf this Christmas night). I thought to myself that into a scene similar to this one, the Savior of the world would be born.

Some fifty-five plus years later, my mind revisited that scene— but from a different perspective. Scripture tells us in Luke 2 of the shepherd's encounter with the angel Gabriel and of the heavenly chorus announcing Jesus' birth. He pointed the direction to the shepherds who agreed that they should go to Bethlehem to witness this event. But my question is, *Did* all *of the shepherds go?* Although a startling experience, it is not clear that *all* of the shepherds followed the angel's instructions. The Bible doesn't say, but my guess is not. Some would have stayed behind. They may have still been afraid after this incredible experience. Or they could have been more concerned about the family business, because, after all, these sheep were their livelihood, and it was their responsibility for the well-being of the flock. They were just kids and must have been curious to see the rest of this story unfold (but, what about the sheep?). Or perhaps there were logistical issues; the flock was too big to move, or, *How do we know there is sufficient grazing or water at this unknown destination*, and, *You expect us to move them at night? What about wild animals or thieves?* There is both safety and security in the fold.

Even though they were clearly pointed to the Savior, perhaps some let "life" get in the way.

And what about the wise men? "Bearing gifts, they traveled *afar*." *Afar* is Hebrew for *a really long way riding on a camel*. Or is it Greek? Actually neither; the songwriter needed something to rhyme with *are*. Regardless, they did travel a really long way with their kingly entourage, which was a major commitment of time (months), resources, and giving up comfort to which they were accustomed. What if they had given up due to the distance or the unknown because they didn't have all of the information? What if they got distracted because of other priorities or started second-guessing about what giving their gifts may cost them in the long term? Bringing gifts requires commitment, deserves our best, and means giving up comfort.

Like those ancient wise men, have you spent a long time seeking the Savior? Or, having found Him, have you brought Him your best gifts?

What an all-inclusive event that Christmas morn; from the most humble station of a shepherd to the regal position of king, all were pointed to Emmanuel—God with us! A God who came for everyone—for me and for you!

So where will life's path lead you in the coming year? Thank you again for walking with me and for your faithful prayers as we successfully pass another marker on my journey of faith.

Seek the Lord while he may be found; call on him while he is near. (Isaiah 55:6)

CARINGBRIDGE® JOURNAL ENTRY #51
JANUARY 27, 2018

WALKING (FALLING) WITH GRACE

I t was the coldest day of the year. The temperature outside was a frigid ten degrees with a wind-chill hovering near zero. A mixture of sleet and light snow from earlier in the day had temporarily thawed but had since frozen again into a solid covering of ice. Reaching for the TV remote, I turned off the ten o'clock local weather report and determined to make my way to the confines of our bedroom where my wife and our warm, comfortable bed awaited me—a thankful refuge from the deadly elements outside. As I rose from the sofa, that's when I first sensed that something was awry. A sharp stabbing pain to my diaphragm . . . another to my back. My breathing became necessarily shallow because every attempt to draw deeper breaths was answered by another stabbing pain.

After a few moments, I mentally convinced myself to *walk it off* (as we guys sometimes have a tendency to do. What? Don't blame me . . . I learned it from my wife and daughters!). I began pacing around the house, pausing to peer out the front door at the frozen tundra that was the street in front of our house. No traffic; no one in their right mind would be out in a mess like this. I resumed my walk with little relief. I climbed the stairs . . . not really sure why . . . only to return downstairs with confirmation of the painful sensations I had before. Nothing debilitating, just not right. If it were a balmy spring night, I'd probably have caved and had Lesa drive me to the ER, just to get it checked out. *But not tonight*, I thought. *Not with the conditions outside. I'll just go to bed and hope it's better in the morning.*

Oh, did I mention that it was snow day and sleepover night for the granddaughters at our house? It ranks right up there with winning the Tennessee Lottery for them. As I turned the corner from the hall into our bedroom, I was met with a maze of sleeping bags and blow-up mattresses and a carefully crafted trail leading between little bodies and into the master bath. I managed to navigate my way to get ready for bed and then returned to my place on the far side of the room where I crawled into bed, searching for relief. *If I can just get comfortable, I'll be able to sleep through it*, I thought, knowing that it typically takes me about two minutes to fall asleep.

As I wiggled to find that perfect spot and position, my mind was going down the checklist of heart attack warning signs. Having convinced myself that I could check the box for most of the symptoms (it only takes one), I then began to rationalize the no-go decision to the ER. The weather conditions were too hazardous for southerners, and I didn't want Whitney and Ben to have to get out in it. There's no way that I'll put Lesa behind the wheel under these conditions. Even the fearless emergency responders should not have to deal with this. Finally, after about twenty minutes of mental deliberation and restlessly contorting my body in the bed, I fell into that desired deep sleep.

It was about three hours later (1:35 a.m.) when nature called, and I again found myself carefully tip-toeing through the bedroom obstacle course. Having accomplished the needed bathroom visit, I was two steps into my return trip to bed when I lost consciousness and collapsed to the bathroom floor. Thank God that He graciously guided a fall that missed both glass door and shower walls, avoided granite counter tops, and minimized the impact of an unforgiving tile floor. Later I would recall that it was as if I'd been gently laid on the floor, amazingly avoiding all of the above-mentioned hazards.

The minutes that followed were a blur for me. I awoke first to Lesa by my side, then Whitney who'd driven from her house, then the emergency responders who efficiently performed their skills, and soon I was packed up in the back of the ambulance and en route to the hospital, a normal drive of five minutes. Due to road conditions, we arrived fifteen minutes later.

Thankfully, tests confirmed that I did not experience a heart attack. A CT scan later determined that I had pleural effusion, a body of fluids that had collected in the lining of my lungs, causing the pain and ultimately effecting the fainting spell. I was admitted to the hospital for a procedure the next day, during which they would draw fluid to test and to relieve the discomfort. We were discharged that Sunday night about 10 p.m.

We were eager to return home, because the week ahead had so much in store. On Tuesday, I would meet with my oncologist to discuss beginning yet another chemotherapy regimen. Also, those of you who have been following my journey know that I have been dealing with double vision for sixteen months resulting from a tumor on my optic nerve. The cancerous lesion was successfully dealt with through gamma knife radiation over a year ago, but doctors recommended giving my body the chance to heal on its own and the vision to self-correct before attempting any corrective surgery. With that time having expired with no improvement, surgery was scheduled for Wednesday of that week, and nothing was getting in the way of that procedure.

But . . . the winter storm resumed on Monday, laying a fresh blanket of snow and ice on the partially thawed roadways. Tuesday brought on single-digit temperatures with wind-chills at or below zero. Schools and businesses had again closed, and everyone was encouraged to stay off of the frozen roadways, particularly on secondary streets downtown. Of course, that was exactly where my surgery was to be done. My procedure was scheduled for 6:30 a.m. the following morning, and it was highly impossible that we would be able to navigate morning traffic on black ice and be there in time. So, we got a hotel room only half a mile from the surgery center to improve our chances. Our drive in on late Tuesday afternoon only confirmed our decision to get as close as possible. Overnight, any thawing would be refreezing into a hazardous mess.

Wednesday weather was as advertised. At 6:00 a.m. we headed into the dark and onto the treacherous street. Thankfully my skillful driver and wife cautiously maneuvered us down the hill and to our intended destination. Although I was the only patient that showed up that day, thankfully the doctor, anesthesiologist, and the support staff all made it, and surgery went on as planned.

Words cannot express the joy, relief, and satisfaction I experienced when the post-surgical dressing was removed, and it was clear that "normal" vision was restored. Although then still traumatized from the procedure, my eye would recover in the couple of weeks ahead and even more improvement would be seen.

Another week passed.

This time I recognized the symptoms. Rolling out of bed was a challenge. The pleural effusion was again causing pain and shortness of breath. This time I didn't need to be encouraged—I was headed back to the ER for a repeat of the former procedures: admission to the hospital, thoracentesis (draining of the fluid in the lungs), monitoring, and hopefully some relief, and sending back home. Thankfully those were the results we saw over the last couple of days.

None of us know how our journeys will ultimately play out or the timetable. The events of the last couple of weeks have reminded me once again of how quickly things and conditions change (for bad and for good).

So, seize opportunities as they present themselves. Openly connect with loved ones—as difficult or awkward as it may seem. Attack and accomplish those things that have been procrastinated far too long. Live each day as the blessing that it is intended to be.

And, thanks for walking with me today!

CARINGBRIDGE® JOURNAL ENTRY #52
FEBRUARY 14, 2018

WALKING . . . NO, DRIVING!

I felt like I was sixteen years old again!

OK, in the interest of full disclosure here, the only thing that felt sixteen again was my freedom to drive. Climbing behind the wheel to drive after a sixteen-month hiatus seemed somewhat surreal. Lesa commented the same thing after we again reversed transportation roles—me as chief mobility officer and she as copilot—assignments that we'd both grown accustomed to after forty-one years together. The optic nerve tumor, while having been successfully treated over a year before, apparently had left residual damage that was not reversing itself. Hence, the long-awaited surgery to correct the double vision was successfully performed, and, after a week of recovery, I now found myself as pilot in command of an awe-inspiring Honda minivan ready to launch. (It may say something about my certainty and confidence as I chose this option over the BMW convertible covered and sitting beside it in the garage!)

And it really didn't matter that I was headed to the cancer clinic to begin yet another new chemo regimen. I was *driving* again!

I remember those teenage days leading up to obtaining a driver's license, and they were being strangely revisited as I quickly and awkwardly stumbled through my preflight checklist. Seats adjusted—check. Mirrors—check. Seat belt fastened—check. Visually check surroundings—check. Brake engaged—check. Ignition sequence—*on*!

As much as we scoff over our selection of a minivan over other preferred SUVs (actually our second such choice), it offers some pretty sweet technology to help one out that was not available . . . well . . . "back in the day." A myriad of camera options guide you, caution alarms alert you when it senses objects in your intended path, collision avoidance sensors warn of other vehicles passing on your right and left, and automated braking takes over when you are getting too close to the vehicles ahead. It's almost as if it can drive itself, until you sit in that designated seat and grab the wheel. Then responsibility and ownership sets in.

For over forty-five years I've had a pretty stellar driving record. Looking back over that time, I'm sure it took a while before I "felt as one" with the vehicle I was driving. That is what was missing on this day. I oddly felt as if I had to work too hard at it. I'm sure that in time that will improve as healing continues and I obtain more hours.

I've often commented that the most debilitating thing about my cancer thus far was impaired vision resulting in my inability to drive. I found myself utterly dependent on someone else. I could no longer step into my garage, select a "model of the day," climb in, and within moments, just let the adventure begin. Whether routine, mundane, or essential, the freedom to drive is just that *freeing*!

But what I have also discovered in this brief time of liberation is that it's not just the vision; I was missing the point. If it wasn't the vision, then it is something else that creeps in to take its place.

It's dependency—not on my eyes but on Him. Focus—not on the gift of sight that may come and go for each of us but the eternal, perpetual, unending gift of salvation to all who call upon His name in belief, repentance, and submission.

Where does your dependence lie?

May these words of my mouth and this meditation of my heart be pleasing in your sight, Lord, my Rock and my Redeemer. (Psalm 19:14, emphasis added)

Thanks for walking with me today!

CARINGBRIDGE® JOURNAL ENTRY #53
MARCH 9, 2018

WALKING . . . TO A PLACE I'VE BEEN BEFORE

As when training for a running event, if you trace the same route over and over again, it will become, well, routine. Yes, there are still things about them that makes each individual run unique, but in time the experience you gather from those repetitive training runs prepares you for the bigger event, because you've already been there. The pace times, the hills, the valleys—you can face them all with confidence because you've already witnessed the results before. You may not have won that race, but you finished it. You may not have set a new PR (personal record), but you finished.

So when the neurologist said, "Well, we've found another small lesion in your brain," we took it in stride. He continued. "That's why we do these periodic scans to keep an eye out for things just like this. The good news is that it is small (2 cm) and very well-defined—just a small dot in the deep recesses between the two lobes at the back of your brain. It's slow growing, and we found it early on, so you are not seeing anything symptomatic of it being there. If you agree, we'll do another gamma knife radiation procedure, which should be easier than the one before." (Besides . . . you've already been there.)

I said we took it in stride . . . that may have been a stretch. We were disappointed, yes. It's never fun getting bad news. It's even worse when receiving bad news becomes the norm. But life had prepared us for this day as well as all of the other days leading up to this one.

I thought of some of the challenges that I'd encountered throughout this journey: initial diagnosis, head and neck surgery at MDA, proton therapy treatment, chemotherapy, then recurrence in my lungs, more chemotherapy, immunotherapy, more chemotherapy, discovery of optic nerve (brain) tumor, more chemotherapy, another surgery, and, yes, more chemo. The same God that formed creation from nothing and knew of my maladies long before I did remains in control. So we can remain confident in Him because He's already been there.

So our training runs (walks) currently are preparing us for the gamma knife procedure on the 15th. We want to take this opportunity to thank those of you who have so faithfully walked alongside us from the earliest days since diagnosis . . . now three years ago. Your prayers and faithful support have ministered to us in so many ways. Your comments have encouraged us when we temporarily lost sight of the goal and have helped keep us on track. We are blessed!

Thanks for walking with me today!

I am your God and will take care of you until you are old and your hair is gray. I made you and will care for you; I will give you help and rescue you. (Isaiah 46:4 GNT)

CARINGBRIDGE® JOURNAL ENTRY #54
MARCH 16, 2018

WALKING IN CELEBRATION!

T his post is from Lesa . . .

Dearest friends, family, and faithful prayer warriors,

This past weekend was the Germantown Half Marathon. As we navigated the cones in the road and the numerous closures in our normal routing, I was reminded that three years ago, Mark and Whitney crossed the finish line of this race hand-in-hand. We celebrated another milestone in their marathon races . . . another 13.1 miles. They were "healthy." All was good.

Little did we know that two weeks after this celebration, Mark would be diagnosed with *head and neck cancer*. Another marathon had begun for him. Not a race he had anticipated or trained for. Nevertheless, the starting gun had been fired, and the race course had been mapped—a course that *God* had ordained. And Mark continues to run, *mile after mile*, enduring doctor visits, aches, pains, surgeries, chemo, radiation . . . *cancer*!

Today, three years later, we *celebrate*. Celebrate *cancer*? No. Celebrate *being cancer free*? Sadly, no. We are celebrating that our God has provided endurance for Mark to keep running.

To highlight a few of the things we have seen on the course . . .

- Wonderful doctors
- MDA Cancer Center
- Successful surgery
- Friendships with others running a cancer race
- Coming home cancer free
- Physical healing
- Auburn football (yep—we beat 'Bama. Had to add that one—war eagle)
- Reoccurring cancer in his lungs
- West Cancer Center (for treatment) . . . only a few miles from our home
- Chemotherapy
- Surgery to remove shoulder lesion
- More chemo
- Brain lesion
- Impaired vision
- Gamma knife
- Chemo
- Limited hospital interruptions
- Pleural effusion
- Eye surgery
- Restored vision
- Chemo
- Another brain lesion
- Another gamma knife procedure
- ***Cancer***

The course has also revealed some of the things you may not know. We celebrate . . .

- *Mark has never stayed in bed. He gets up every morning and dresses.* He may not have gotten too far away from the couch but is always up and facing the race course for the day.

- *Mark has not thrown up once.* This is an absolute miracle with all the different kinds of chemo he has tolerated.

- *Mark has reconnected with high school friends, business associates, and so many others* with the aid of modern technology. He is on the prayer lists of sweet friends around the world, including Russia, Africa, and Spain. His CaringBridge® site has recorded over 16,275 visits since it went live in May of 2015.

We have so much to celebrate.

And as we approach Easter, we celebrate our Lord and Savior Jesus Christ. HE IS RISEN! HE IS ALIVE! *He* has been our constant companion on this race. *He* has set the pace for Mark every day. *He* has held our hands on the sharpest curves and tallest hills that Mark has run. *He* has provided *miracles* . . . Mark is alive and surviving cancer. Thank You, Jesus!

We, too, celebrate with thanksgiving for each of you. Thank you for praying, encouraging, and helping with Connie (my sister) and Vanessa (my niece) and other family issues in our times of need. We are blessed! Thank you for loving our family!

Thank you for walking with *us* today!

—**Lesa**

CARINGBRIDGE® JOURNAL ENTRY #55
MAY 19, 2018

WALKING ... TO MY PLACE IN LINE

S pring has sprung to life at our house. Lesa recently discovered a mother mallard duck had made her nest in our front flower bed. Later the duck would lay her eleven eggs in a reasonably small space behind a boxwood and cornered by our front porch.

Also, within feet of that, a pair of house wrens made a nest in the floral arrangement on the front door. Soon six tiny eggs filled the little nest to its brim.

I don't know why these mother birds have chosen the spots they have to give birth. We don't live in a particularly bird friendly area, and our front door is perpetually being opened and closed, no doubt disturbing the incubation and birthing process.

Maybe they'd heard of Lesa's mothering and caregiving skills that have become legendary. And she's taken to them like they were her own—protecting their nests from intruders while keeping a close eye on their progress.

But last week we traveled to Dallas to visit Lindsay and family, and, as nature would have it, while we were away, the ducklings hatched. Neighbors sent us video of what must have been their leaving the nest. They'd crossed the street, and the mother hopped the curb and patiently waited a few feet on the sidewalk while the eleven ducklings tried to figure out how to clear the obstacle that was over twice their height. They could not see the mother, only hear her. After a few moments of mass confusion resembling black ants whose bed had been disrupted, out of the chaos popped the first duckling onto the grass, then another, then another . . . by clumsily working together. This continued until there was only one left—the lone duckling for which there was no one to give a boost.

Though only a couple of days old, it was astounding the degree of intimacy that the mother mallard had for her children. First of all, she knew she had eleven—not five, not seven . . . eleven. She recognized each of them uniquely. So, after sensing that one was missing, she returned to retrieve that remaining duckling before continuing the flock's journey to the river for their first lesson in swimming and feeding on their own.

This week was my scheduled visit to West Cancer Center for labs, a CT scan, and a visit with my oncologist. About ten days before, I'd stopped taking the oral treatment Votrient because of the side effects. So I was feeling good with my system being pretty much drug free.

But that targeted therapy was not achieving the desired results. Scans showed some slight continued progression in my lungs but more aggressive growth in other outlying tumors. After discussing options with Dr. Portnoy, we mutually concluded that my cancer was not responding to sarcoma-based treatment, and my case should be referred back to Dr. Al Weir (my former oncologist who specializes in head and neck cancers) to once again pursue a carcinoma-based approach. So, after meeting with Dr. Weir, the decision was made to basically start over—beginning with another biopsy (coming up this Tuesday) and then charting a new course from there.

At times I feel like that last duckling in the line . . . struggling to keep up with the others, finding it nearly impossible to muscle myself up and over obstacles without assistance, finding myself at the rear of the flock and not able to see what lies ahead but rather blindly following the procession immediately in front of me.

The difference is that my blind faith lies not in earthly instruction or example. We are resolved that God has this and will make Himself known for His glory!

Oh, I almost forgot . . . the six house wren eggs hatched too. They continue to fatten up due to the frequent feedings of their parents. It won't be long before they stretch their wings and demonstrate their own faith to take flight for the first time. And we'll be empty nesters once again.

> *Now faith is confidence in what we hope for and assurance about what we do not see. (Hebrews 11:1)*

Thanks for walking with me today!

CARINGBRIDGE® JOURNAL ENTRY #56
JUNE 22, 2018

WALKING WITH A BLOOD CLOT

The pain wasn't debilitating but rather unsettling. It was reminiscent of the pleural effusions that had twice landed me in the hospital to have the fluid drawn from my lungs. We'd traveled eight hours to attend the funeral of a dear friend and mentor who had died two days after his ninety-fifth birthday. I was to be a pallbearer at the service the next day. But after checking in to the hotel, unloading our bags, and returning the luggage cart, Lesa read me and knew something was amiss.

"I'm OK . . . just feel that maybe another pleural effusion is coming on," I said.

"That's it," she replied. "We're driving back to Memphis."

There are two things that I have learned through this battle with cancer: listen to my body and listen to my wife (not necessarily in that order!). With a sense of urgency and caution, we retraced the eight hours back home to where the medical staff was familiar with my case. After a restful night in my own bed, the pain still lingered, and early the following morning, we headed to the emergency room. A battery of tests followed. Before long, the attending ER physician came into the room.

"I hate to tell you this, but you have a serious situation. In all my thirty-three years of practicing medicine, I have never seen anything like it. You have a tumor growing inside your pulmonary vein, leading from your lungs to your heart (*this we knew*). But a blood clot has also formed at that site (*this we didn't know*). You don't have pleural effusion . . . it's the blood clot and tumor that's causing your pain. We are admitting you for further evaluation."

Later that evening and after receiving pain meds, my pain had subsided, and I felt good as new again. But I would spend the following three days in the hospital with the hospitalist, my oncologist, and the cardiologist, all agreeing as to the severity of my condition. Should a piece of that tumor break off or if the blood clot should dislodge, either could produce deadly results. A blood thinner was prescribed to lessen those chances. I was sent home and told not to overly exert myself.

That was last week, and I have felt fine going about my normal routine. This week began with an MRI scan to evaluate the effectiveness of the gamma knife radiation treatment that I had ninety days ago for the latest brain lesion. Because my neurologist was out of the office the day I had my scan, results would be given by phone after he returned to the office and had a chance to review the findings.

For a three-year cancer survivor such as myself, the MRI drill becomes somewhat routine. After selecting one's choice of music to listen to, you lay down on the hard gurney/table surface that will convey you back a few feet into the instrument. The choice of music is nothing more than an attempt to relax the patient from the somewhat intimidating procedure. But once the machine is activated, the hammering of the magnetic equipment overrides any attempt to hear the music. Even though you have on ear protection to save your hearing, you can't tell if they are playing hard rock, country, or southern gospel. So you try your best to let your mind go to another place.

I found myself reflecting on how blessed I was to have grown up during a time when God, the Bible, prayer, and patriotism were an integral part of education and school life. Each day began with the pledge of allegiance. Teachers and administrators openly prayed at assemblies and, on occasion, in the classroom. In my case, memorizing scriptures was a mandatory part of the second-grade curriculum. My teacher, Mrs. McEachin, required that we memorized and individually recited select scriptures. Among those were Psalm 23 and Psalm 100. Beyond learning and reciting those passages when called on, there wasn't a lot that I understood about how this applied to my life as a second grader. But it had profound meaning to me over half a century later as I perfectly recalled those words from David in Psalm 23:

> *The Lord is my shepherd, I lack nothing.*
> *He makes me lie down in green pastures,*
> *he leads me beside quiet waters,*
> *he refreshes my soul.*
> *He guides me along the right paths*
> *for his name's sake.*
> *Even though I walk through the darkest valley,*
> *I will fear no evil,*
> *for you are with me;*
> *your rod and your staff,*
> *they comfort me.*
>
> *You prepare a table before me*
> *in the presence of my enemies.*
> *You anoint my head with oil;*
> *my cup overflows.*
> *Surely your goodness and love will follow me*
> *all the days of my life,*
> *and I will dwell in the house of the LORD*
> *forever.*

(That's a lot of big words for a second grader.)

As the MRI machine pounded and pounded away, I continued to repeat those words in my head with precision. In retrospect, I only remember two things about the second grade:

1. Mrs. McEachin sharing with us that President John F. Kennedy had died and

2. memorizing those scriptures.

That seed, planted fifty-five years ago, continues to bear fruit, with understanding today in this time of need.

I also met with my oncologist this week to determine the next course of treatment for my cancer. We will begin with an oral medication that promises to be less punishing on me than previous treatments.

Oh, and as Lesa and I were out biking in the neighborhood this morning, the neurologist's office called with the MRI results. After reviewing the scans, he "has some concerns" and wants me to come in to discuss. But that is next week. And so the story continues . . .

Thanks for walking with me today!

CARINGBRIDGE® JOURNAL ENTRY #57
JULY 18, 2018

WALKING AND LOOKING BACK

O K, let's stop for a moment. We've just made it up the most recent hill, and this presents a great time for us to take stock of our blessings. Look back down this hill with me and see how many people are faithfully walking with us on this journey. It is indeed our own marathon. If you are still one of those who have read and responded to the CaringBridge® updates since the inception of my site, then you have been a faithful training partner with me now *for over three years*! I can't begin to thank you enough! Your words of encouragement, and most of all, your prayers, have enabled us to press on through the times of difficulty that we have faced . . . together.

One of the really neat things about being on CaringBridge® is that I am able to go back and review not only my journal posts but also your individual responses to me in a confidential fashion. I paused last week to review a segment of those responses dating back to our earliest days of walking together. Your comments are just as meaningful now as they were then and in some cases even more so because I have the retrospect of being able to look back down those hills of struggles and have experienced victory.

But as I poured over those responses, I also was reminded of those friends and loved ones who began this journey and faithfully walked alongside us who are no longer with us. While it was "just three years ago" when this journey started, I was amazed at the number of names that made up that list—a stark reminder of our own mortalities and of the urgency to seek God's salvation *now*!

Others have just gotten tired of the walk; after all, three years is more than any of us originally signed up for. So for those of you who continue on with me, bless you, and I pray that this exercise in endurance proves helpful, regardless of the battle you may be facing.

When I last posted three weeks ago, I left you hanging regarding the results of my brain MRI. Good news is that the previous two gamma knife radiation treatments seemed to have worked with no apparent growth at those sites. Bad news is that there were three new lesions in my brain, and while they are small (less than one millimeter), they still needed to be addressed. I opted for another gamma knife procedure, which I underwent last week. It was routine except for the fact that I went in expecting them to address only three places, and after doing the MRI in preparation for the procedure, they found another two really small ones, which they were able to take care of during this session. Because they had to figure dosage and treatment plans for five different locations, I was on the table for over five hours. A couple of days for the sedation medication to wear off, and I was back to my not-so-normal self. And I have resumed my latest chemo after dialing up the dosage. Fortunately I am able to take it orally every day at home and am not tethered to the clinic for treatments by infusion. *See, there's goodness and blessings in everything if you only dig deep enough!*

Thanks again for walking with me today and for the other eleven-hundred-plus days since our journey began!

I remain confident of this: I will see the goodness of the Lord in the land of the living. Wait for the Lord; be strong and take heart and wait for the Lord. (Psalm 27:13-14)

THE FINAL CHAPTER

There is a road that we all must walk. There is no GPS for the tech savvy, no road map for the directionally challenged, and no highway signs to help you to reach that final destination. It's the road that leads to eternity. Rand McNally does not offer an atlas, and a Google search can't get you there. It's where all roads reach their earthly end. For some of us, that road will be long . . . and for others, it will end far too soon in our human perspective.

As I began this journey of faith, I turned this malady over to the Lord for Him to use as He saw fit to bring honor and glory to Him. Whether in life extended through His healing or an outcome resulting in death, I had no idea that the prayer I uttered that day in downtown Memphis over three years ago would result in the writing of this book. I had always told myself that I had a book in me, and it was something that I would love to do, but I never knew what the subject would be. But as the journal entries in CaringBridge® began to accumulate, it became clear that this may be my last opportunity to point others to Christ in a meaningful way.

Throughout the journey and its numerous turns, hills, valleys, and unexpected disappointments, I prayed that God would grant me the remaining days sufficient to both complete it and to get the book published—not for my own gratification but that the story could be finished. And it seemed that every time I would make that request, days, weeks, and sometimes months would go by without a single page being written. Maybe it was my way of selfishly trying to grab the reigns back and steer to the path that I preferred.

But reality remains: *I am dying!*

I don't know the details as to when, where, or how that will all play out, but that is something that both you and I have in common. Every breath we take, every beat of our heart takes us one step further from the things we know and love here on earth and one step closer to eternity.

My question for you is, *Are you prepared to face eternity?* It is the single most important decision that you will face in your lifetime. More important than choosing a mate, pursuing an education, determining a career path, or chasing that dream that you are convinced will "bring fulfillment." More important than all the things you can amass or the wealth you can manage to accumulate. Your future destiny and eternity hangs in the balance.

Some people will deny the existence of God and an afterlife and face death with a "when it's over, it's over" mindset. If you are in this camp, I hasten to tell you that you are wrong. The same God that created this earth and filled it with wonder and beauty for us to enjoy has prepared a heavenly home for those who believe in Him— an eternal home that defies our earthly imaginations. The same God that sent His only Son, Jesus, to live a life of example for us for thirty-three years and then loved us enough to allow Him to die an excruciating death as payment for the sins of everyone in this fallen world. And as if that were not enough, He offers eternal life to all who believe in Him.

Or maybe you are relying on your goodness (relative to others) to earn your way into the presence of God. The Bible tells us that "all have sinned and fall short of the glory of God" (Romans 3:23). But it's not a matter of being a good man (religious or not) that will ultimately count when we face our Maker. I am guilty of a laundry list of sins, which has left me far short of the expectation that He has for me to live a truly "good" life. Though, while I am not good in His eyes, *I am forgiven.* There's nothing good that I could have done to earn that forgiveness; it's a free gift. It's a gift that is available to everyone who calls on His name, confesses their sins and unworthiness, and through faith accepts His forgiveness. It is only through Jesus that we have ultimate HOPE.

Or perhaps you attend church occasionally or at least recognize Christmas and Easter as times that you should be there as a way to "have your ticket punched." While frequent church attendance with fellow believers is important for growth and fellowship and to further the cause of Christ here on earth, it alone is not what God intended for a personal relationship with us.

Others choose to take a position of "one day I'll get around to it"; it's on our perpetual *to-do list* and is one of those items that continues to get carried forward because it is not a high enough priority to us to handle today. First of all, *there is no higher priority.* Show me where you have a guarantee of breathing even one more breath or having one more flawless heartbeat. This is *your* wake-up call. Don't delay! "Here's your sign." "Just do it!" *Now.*

Please understand that I don't profess to know all of the answers—all of the hows or the whys. I don't know what path lies ahead, as it has already taken some strange turns. What I do know is that my God is walking that path with me, leading me with a peace that will sustain me throughout these trials. I've already seen how so many of the prayers that have been lifted up on my behalf are being answered. And there will be more . . .

So, this is where our journey together will end, for now. But you must walk on, confident in the fact that you are never alone, with faith to face each new day—each day that is a good gift! So rejoice in it, never allowing anyone or anything to rob you of your joy.

You go on ahead now. You've been a faithful companion as we have walked together. But I need some rest. And remember, for me, all of this has just been . . . a temporary inconvenience.

CPSIA information can be obtained
at www.ICGtesting.com
Printed in the USA
BVHW041349070119
537204BV00013B/672/P